Contents

Preface

Half a century ago Joseph Hone very properly warned all concerned not to attach too much importance to the influence of Schopenhauer upon George Moore. The advice remains as sound as it was in 1936, although today we are probably more likely to attach too little importance to the subject. It is, however, time to investigate Moore's attitude towards the philosopher whom his friend and enemy W.B. Yeats called 'my sainted Schopenhauer', and indeed towards German philosophy in general. The idea of 'Kant' Moore studying the 'specious sophistries of German philosophers', as he very kindly called them, puts one in mind of Thomas Love Peacock's Mr. Flosky plunging into the 'central opacity of Kantian metaphysics'; no doubt Rev. Dr. Follicott spoke for Peacock himself — and for George Moore too, come to that — when he remarked that Kant 'wants the two great requisites of head and tail.' Think what we will of 'Kant' Moore, his *Schopenhaueriste* and *Zarathoustran* poses both reveal much of the man behind the mask, or at least behind these particular masks. Any study of George Moore is necessarily concerned with the man and his masks; this is part of the fascination of the subject. It may no longer be possible to take the 'man-of-letters' seriously, but as writer and human being Moore remains a wholly plausible figure. His very whimsicality, his pronunciamentos and recantations, his mixture of self-importance and self-doubt, self-magnification and self-parody, pugnaciousness and prudence, are all too human. And then there is the question of when he is speaking the truth, which involves the further question of what he means by truth, and the fact that he clearly understands the term in what Nietzsche calls an extra-moral sense. If he occasionally deviates from what most others would regard as the truth, he does so for what Schopenhauer regarded as the usual reason: because he is trying to ensure himself his readers' respect. 'Face' is important to him. Truth may therefore be a matter not only of aesthetics, of what sounds best, but of *braggadocio*. That said, the reader has continually to guard against taking literally what is not meant literally. Moore's provocative-sounding pronouncements, often dramatized into conversations, may be no more than moments in his creative stream of consciousness; what sounds dogmatically absolute when taken out of context, is relativized and ironized by the context. These pronouncements are problematical if taken literally as the pompous pronunciamentos of a pundit; they are more interesting and more revealing if regarded as manifestations of the secret difficulties of the creative artist, for Moore's trumpetings against 'ideas' reflect his problems and self-doubts at moments when he becomes conscious of the dangers of subjectivity. If he is accordingly often in danger of being misjudged, the reader is no less often in danger of misjudging him. He is nothing if not stimulating company.

For the reader's convenience I have treated bibliographical references in two ways: page-references to primary material are given in brackets in the text, while all other references are relegated to the notes. In references I have used abbreviated titles for Schopenhauer's works: *P&P* (= *Parerga and Paralipomena*) and *WWI* (= *The World as Will and Idea*).

My debts will mostly be obvious. No one can write about Schopenhauer in France without being much indebted to R.-P. Colin, and no one can work on George Moore without returning, again and again, to Joseph Hone's biography. My greatest debt, however, is to Jean Noël, not only because his *George Moore. L'homme et l'oeuvre* remains the most valuable and substantial of all studies of Moore's work, but because he has given so generously of his time and so liberally of his invariably judicious advice.

I. Schopenhauer à *la mode*

George Moore was not, of course, the first English-language man of letters to discover Schopenhauer, for that is a distinction that belongs first to John Oxenford and then to William James. Nor was he the first novelist to express a philosophy that has been seen as indebted to Schopenhauer, for that more dubious distinction belongs to Thomas Hardy. Nor was he the novelist who took Schopenhauer most seriously, for that was unquestionably George Gissing. The story of his relationship to Schopenhauer is, however, amusing and instructive, well worth the telling.

In preparing the third edition of the *Confessions of a Young Man* for publication in 1889, Moore added to the first and second editions of 1888 some sixty pages for which he made an extraordinary claim. In the Preface to the third edition he wrote:

> These additions, though they do not amount in all to above sixty pages, seem to me of the utmost importance; for they enabled me to accentuate the philosophy of the book (that of Schopenhauer), that philosophy which alone helps us to live while in the evil of living, that philosophy which alone shows us the real good and leads us from the real evil. I owe much of my mind to Schopenhauer.

But how serious was Moore in his claim to owe 'much of his mind' to Schopenhauer in 1889? Did he really believe this to be true? And, more to the point, was it true? There are many good reasons for treating any statement by Moore with the greatest caution, let alone one made in the preface to a fictionalized autobiography which reveals nothing more clearly than its author's characteristic unwillingness to distinguish between fact and fiction. Truth, for George Moore, was essentially an aesthetic phenomenon.

In order to test the truth of Moore's claim we need to go back to the first and second editions of the *Confessions* to see whether their philosophy is 'that of Schopenhauer'. It could be, since by this time Moore had already published three novels (*A Drama in Muslin*, 1886; *A Mere Accident*, 1887; *Spring Days*, 1888) in which there are echoes of Schopenhauer's philosophy, and was about to publish a fourth (*Mike Fletcher*, 1889). Clearly he had some knowledge of Schopenhauer. But how much? Did he read Schopenhauer? Where did he come across him? And what did he make of him?

Moore did not read German, and German literature was not his strong point. In the early days he is said not to have known his Schiller from his Schopenhauer, and as late as 1906 it was because he professed to 'know nothing of German literature' (*Salve*, XIV) that he resolved to consult Kuno

Meyer on the subject. Meyer told him that Schopenhauer was among the great German writers, which Moore must have already known. While he took both Schopenhauer and Nietzsche relatively seriously, and Wagner rather more seriously, this is more than can be said of Goethe. Moore's autobiographical writings carry the obligatory references to Goethe, whom he calls 'the wisest man since Antiquity' (ibid, VII), but they are not convincing. Goethe's 'sane and massive paganism' cut no ice with George Moore, who was evidently irked by what he regarded as Goethe's self-importance. In *Avowals* (1919; repr. Ebury Edition 1936, 123f., 191f.) Moore speaks of Goethe as 'pompous' and 'prone to make mystery by muddying pure water' (whatever that is supposed to mean); the *Italian Journey* he describes as 'a pompous, empty narrative of a journey in Italy, lacking character, life and movement: the sort of book that our fathers and grandfathers were wont to put together when they returned home from the grand tour.' How George Gissing would have objected to this! However, a remark in Chapter VIII of *Conversations in Ebury Street* ('Was it not Goethe who said that we cease to be original the moment we come into the world? an aphorism which I have never been able to accept, perhaps because I do not know the context'), shows that Moore knew virtually nothing of Goethe.

And then there is Moore's story of his Kant phase:

> I had only just turned eighteen, and was deeply interested in religious problems, and one day I told her [Mrs Colville Bridger] the book I carried in my pocket, and sometimes pretended to study, was Kant's *Critique of Pure Reason*. My explanation of the value of the work did not seem to strike her . . . One day in the greenhouse, whither I had wandered, she interrupted some allusion to the chapter entitled, 'The Deduction of the Categories,' with a burst of laughter, and declared that she would call me Kant . . . she held to the name . . . and during the course of our long friendship never addressed me by any other. (*Memoirs of My Dead Life*, *X*: 'A Remembrance').

The idea of 'Kant' Moore, with his well-known aversion to reading, studying the *Critique of Pure Reason*, of all things, is not a likely story, although Moore was evidently delighted with it; in his *Confessions of a Young Man* he included a more apocryphal-sounding and yet more plausible version: 'While I was waiting for my coach to take a party of *tarts* and *mashers* to the Derby, I would read a chapter of Kant, and I often took the book away with me in my pocket.' Moore does, however, admit that he only 'sometimes pretended to study' Kant, unlike the autobiographical hero of the *Confessions*, who naturally makes a more impressive story out of it: 'Shelley's atheism had led me to read Kant, Spinoza, Godwin, Darwin, and Mill' (*Confessions*, 2nd Edn. 1888, 13). George Moore's interest in Kant was most likely aroused by the book, *A Treatise on the Art of Reasoning*, in which his grandfather and namesake, whom Moore liked to call an 'agnostic', attacked Kant and 'the new German philosophy' for denying the existence of proofs for a personal God. The fruits of George Moore's reading of Kant may well have been the 'We know nothing' of his Sir Owen Asher (*Evelyn Innes*, 1898, 392); if so, this would help to account for his extraordinary aversion to anything smacking of an idea. One recalls that Pater, in his 'Winckelmann' essay, noted that Kant's influence over the culture of Goethe consisted in a severe limitation to the concrete. While it would be unwise to speculate at any length about the impact on George Moore of a complex philosopher whose work he had only pretended to study, it will hardly be wide of the mark to say that his pretended study of Kant will have tended to confirm him in his atheism and in his view of truth as an aesthetic category. A reference in *Confessions of a Young Man* (1904 Edn., 231) to the 'profound greyness of Hegelism' tends in the same direction; it is unlikely to reflect any first-hand knowledge of Hegel, and almost certainly goes back to a reading of Schopenhauer, who in the Fourth Book ('Denial of the Will to Live') of *The World as Will and Idea* speaks of 'Hegelism, that school of dullness, that centre of misunderstanding and ignorance, that mind-destroying, spurious wisdom'. This brings us to the real question: whether Moore also only pretended to study Schopenhauer.

Knowing no German, Moore was not in a position to read Schopenhauer until the first French and English translations appeared, although he could have obtained a good general introduction to Schopenhauer's ideas from published sources in both England and France. The English sources include John Oxenford's famous 'Iconoclasm in German Philosophy' (*Westminster Review*, April 1853), Francis Hueffer's 'Arthur Schopenhauer' (*Fortnightly Review*, December 1876), Helen Zimmern's *Arthur Schopenhauer. His Life and his Philosophy* (1876), Francis Bowen's *Modern Philosophy from Descartes to Schopenhauer and Hartmann* (1877), and James Sully's *Pessimism* (1877; French edition, 1882). There is, however, no reason to suppose that Moore knew any of these works, with the possible exception of Bowen's book, which he may have come across in the early 1880s. Sully's *Pessimism* includes an account of Schopenhauer's philosophy, but there is nothing in that account which suggests that Moore may have known it; besides, from 1873 to 1880 he was in Paris, which is where our enquiry must begin.

Shortly after Moore arrived in Paris there appeared the first monograph on Schopenhauer to be published in France: Théodule Ribot, *La philosophie de Schopenhauer* (1874). This influential work was followed, in 1877, by the first French translation of a complete work by Schopenhauer, *Essai sur le libre-arbitre* (tr. S. Reinach). In 1879 there was another one: *Le fondement de la morale* (tr. Auguste Burdeau). There had been some half a dozen earlier translations of Schopenhauer into French in the years 1856–1870, but these were short extracts which mostly appeared in periodicals that were relatively obscure, at least so far as literary circles were concerned: the most noteworthy was probably A. Maillard's version of the 'Métaphysique d'amour' which appeared in the *Revue Germanique* on 31 January 1861.

When Flaubert wrote to Mme Roger des Genettes on 13 June 1879: 'Connaissez-vous Schopenhauer? J'en lis deux livres',[1] he will have been referring to Reinach's and Burdeau's translations. In theory Moore could have read Ribot's book and Reinach's and Burdeau's translations; in practice there is no evidence that he did so. In 1880 there appeared a selection from *Parerga und Paralipomena* entitled *Aphorismes sur la sagesse dans la vie* (tr. J.A. Cantacuzène). The first French version of Schopenhauer's major work, *Le Monde comme Volonté et comme Représentation* (tr. J.A. Cantacuzène) appeared in two volumes in 1886. Another translation (by Auguste Burdeau) appeared in three volumes in 1888–1890.

Ironically it was another work published in 1880, the year in which Moore left Paris, which was to be so important in this context. This work, Jean Bourdeau's *Schopenhauer. Pensées, maximes et fragments*, which consisted of translations of the 'Metaphysics of Love' and 'On Women', not only made of Schopenhauer a Gallic philosopher; it led to a Schopenhauer cult which, from 1880 to 1886, far surpassed its slightly later English equivalent. In his Preface Bourdeau noted that Schopenhauer was already 'dans toutes les bouches; on le commente dans les chaires de philosophie, on le cite dans les salons.' Confirmation of the truth of this is given by the fact that Brunetière published on 15 January 1879, in the *Revue des Deux Mondes*, an article on the subject of 'le Schopenhauerismus' (which is defined as 'rien . . . qu'une transformation de la philosophie de l'égoïsme').[2] We need look no further than these salons for Moore's first introduction to the fashionable pessimist, for many of the ideas in his work clearly come from the public domain, the cafés and salons of the day.

Although Ribot's book was not without effect, it was Bourdeau's edition which caused Schopenhauer to be greeted as a saint and a god. The result was that by the mid-1880s Paris was positively infested with *Schopenhaueristes*. The type was amusingly described in a mock Theophrastan character by Albert Millaud[3] which appeared in *Le Figaro* on Sunday 21 March 1886:

LE SCHOPENHAUERISTE

Un type nouveau. C'est le philosophe homme du monde, aimant le plaisir, fréquentant les salons et les théâtres, ayant bon estomac; mais jouant au blasé, au désillusionné, au dégoûté. Le nom de Schopenhauer lui a plu; il l'a adopté et mis à la mode. Schopenhauer est devenu pour lui comme une espèce de tailleur moral, de chapelier transcendant, de bottier métaphysique. Il s'est Schopenhauerisé comme on se morphinise, par genre.

Le Schopenhaueriste n'est donc pas un misanthrope. C'est un pessimiste. Il s'amuse avec tristesse, il cause avec mélancolie, il rit avec désespoir. S'il mange des truffes, il vous dit qu'il en aura du mal à l'estomac. S'il boit du vieux vin, il est sûr d'en garder une abominable migraine. Dans le mariage il ne voit que le divorce, dans l'amour il ne voit que la trahison. De tout cela, il ne pense pas un mot et il serait incapable d'expliquer ses idées. Mais il est de chic d'être triste, maussade et d'être en proie aux *blue devils*, comme disent les Anglais. Schopenhauer lui fournit les éléments nécessaires pour affecter ces façons lugubres.

Le Schopenhaueriste joue dans les salons le rôle du *Médecin malgré lui*. 'Savez-vous le latin?' dit Sganarelle à Géronte. — 'Non', répond celui-ci. 'Alors, *Rosa*, la rose, *gloria*, la gloire, *Dominus*, le Seigneur', etc. De même le Schopenhaueriste: 'Avez-vous lu Schopenhauer?' demande-t-il. — 'Non, monsieur.' Alors, il hausse les épaules, il vous plaint, il vous méprise et il vous explique que vous ne savez pas grand'chose, si vous ne savez pas ce que c'est que Schopenhauer.

Règle générale. Le Schopenhaueriste n'a jamais lu Schopenhauer.

This Schopenhauerization of Parisian fashionable intellectual society went, it seems, to such extraordinary lengths that

le fait est que voilà assez longtemps qu'elle nous enschopenhauerde l'enschopenhauerante école d'extatiques de Schopenhauer, le doux M. Paul Bourget en tête . . .

Si la psychologie est devenue pour les invalides de la vie contemporaine ce qu'était la dévotion pour les vieilles femmes d'il y a trente ans, tout s'explique et tout s'arrange: il y a quelques années encore, une femme se découvrait des cheveux blancs et des rides; elle remisait son éventail, ouvrait un Evangile et prenait un confesseur; aujourd'hui elle garde son éventail, ouvre Schopenhauer et reçoit M. Paul Bourget à sa table . . . Oh! la psychologie et les *pièces psychologiques*! oh! ces Schopenhauerdeurs et Schopenhauerdants![4]

The *Schopenhaueriste* 's'amuse avec tristesse, il cause avec mélancholie, il rit avec désespoir',[5] but has almost invariably not read a word of Schopenhauer. Is it even remotely conceivable that the young George Moore would not have been immensely impressed with such specimens? Surely not, especially when one remembers that he must have been familiar with the name of Schopenhauer before 1886. The truth of the matter is that the Theophrastan character of the *Schopenhaueriste* fits 'pagan Moore' like a glove. The *Schopenhaueriste*, in the sense of the female of the species (which Moore appears to have been fortunate enough not to meet), featured in Edouard Pailleron's comedy *Le Monde òu l'on s'ennuie*, which opened at the Comédie Française on 25 April 1881. There was considerable speculation at the time as to the real-life models for the principal figures of the piece. Who the *Schopenhaueriste* Lucy Watson was supposed to represent, is no longer known, but the 'savant à la mode', Professor Bellac, was taken to represent Elme Caro, a fashionable academic philosopher who appeared at all the best salons and was the author of *Le pessimisme au XIXe siècle* (1878). Whether Moore met Elme Caro, I do not know; by his own accounts he should have done since he claimed to move in the same circles. The play might equally well have been called 'L'Anglaise et le professeur', for it revolves around a young English blue stocking named Lucy Watson, 'une jeune fille qui a des lunettes et qui n'a pas de gorge . . . une pédante qui . . . traduit Schopenhauer', and *professeur de salon* Bellac. It is not true that Lucy 'n'a pas de gorge': when she appears *en grande toilette décolletée* in Act I, Scene VIII, the Duchess comments: 'C'est n'est pourtant pas pour le nommé Schopenhauer que vous avez fait cette toilette-là, j'imagine?' She is, of course, right. Bellac's lectures on comparative literature evidently derive in part from Schopenhauer, for Mme de Loudan chides him: 'il n'y a qu'une chose [in his lecture] que je n'accepte pas, c'est que l'amour ait sa raison dans l'instinct.' That this is an echo of 'The Metaphysics of Love' is confirmed when Lucy adds 'Il ne s'agit ici, ni du bien, ni du mal, . . . mais de l'existence même de l'espèce.' When Bellac falls for Lucy, he doesn't know which leg to hop on. Speaking at a salon of 'une certaine philosophie qui fait de l'instinct la base et la règle de toutes nos actions et de toutes nos pensées', he hastens to add that 'cette opinion n'est pas la mienne.' Lofty souls, it seems, do not love as others do. But when Lucy makes it clear that she has no time for the alternative Platonic love, Bellac has to admit that he too is a creature of instinct. The comedy, in other words, revolves around that part of Bourdeau's volume which most impressed French readers when it came out in 1880: 'The Metaphysics of Love.' Whether Moore saw the play, I do not know, but he must have heard of it.

In the early 1880s, then, Schopenhauer reigned supreme not only in fashionable Paris, but in Parisian literary circles. Among the *Médanistes* there was for a time *none* who was not under his sway, and Bourdeau's edition was read by all the members of the Médan group, with the possible exception of Léon Hennique; Schopenhauer left his mark on the work of Zola, Huysmans, Maupassant, Céard, Alexis and Rod. Rémy de Gourmont was fully justified in writing, in the context of an essay on Villiers de l'Isle-Adam, that 'Notre éducation philosophique, à quelques-uns, avait . . . été faite par le "Schopenhauer" de M. Bourdeau et celui de M. Ribot. Nous avions déjà découvert, et avec quelle ivresse, à la fois que le monde était mauvais et qu'il n'existait que relativement à nous-mêmes.'[6] It is, of course, to Moore's generation that this admirable comment applies. Not surprisingly, it was Schopenhauer's pessimism, rather than his philosophical idealism, which attracted the naturalists; Colin has made that point well: 'Les naturalistes, à dire le vrai, avaient montré peu d'intérêt pour l'idéalisme schopenhauerien. La dénonciation brillante des maux terrestres avait bien davantage retenu leur attention, attirée également par la morale du pessimiste.'[7] What makes this significant in our context is the fact that the *Médanistes* were Moore's most important literary contacts, idols and models during this period, when he continued to visit Paris regularly and frequently.

Of all the Médan group it was his 'old friend' Paul Alexis whom Moore knew best. It was Alexis who accompanied him when he went to visit Zola, Alexis of whom he wrote so charmingly in 'La Butte' (*Memoirs of My Dead Life*). The title of Alexis' collection of stories, *Le Besoin d'Amour* (1885), is taken from Schopenhauer's 'Metaphysics of Love', as Alexis himself wrote to Zola on 15 September 1883.[8] In an article entitled 'L'Amour' published in *Le Rèveil* on 5 August 1883 Alexis quoted extensively from the 'Metaphysics of Love', including Schopenhauer's view that love is the final goal of almost every human effort. By the time he accompanied Moore to Médan in

1882, he had probably already read Bourdeau's book, his attention having been drawn to it by Céard or by Zola himself. In Alexis Moore therefore had a possible source of information on Schopenhauer.

The real *Schopenhaueriste* among the *Médanistes* was, however, Maupassant, who wrote on 17 April 1880 in *Le Gaulois*: 'Je trouve que Schopenhauer et Herbert Spencer ont sur la vie beaucoup d'idées plus droits que l'illustre auteur des *Misérables*'. Maupassant knew Jean Bourdeau and was one of the first readers of his Schopenhauer selection. He probably also read Cantacuzène's *Aphorismes* in 1880. Maupassant's profound admiration for his 'maître', Schopenhauer, is well attested; it is first seen in 'Les dimanches d'un bourgeois de Paris' (31 May – 18 August 1880), in which Schopenhauer appears as 'un grand philosophe'; the passage on women, which unduly impressed George Moore, is quoted from Bourdeau: 'ce sexe de petite taille, aux épaules étroites, aux larges hanches et aux jambes courtes'. It was Schopenhauer's view of woman which was the subject of an article by Maupassant entitled 'La Lysistrata moderne' which appeared in *Le Gaulois* on 30 December 1880;[9] his attitude is put most forcibly in a letter to Gisèle d'Estoc in which he wrote, in January 1881: 'J'admire éperdument Schopenhauer et sa théorie de l'amour me semble la seule acceptable'.[10] Notwithstanding his low opinion of Maupassant ('Maupassant ... seemed to me too much like an intrigue with a housemaid': *Vale*), we shall see that Moore, too, liked to quote Schopenhauer's view of Woman. Not surprisingly, Maupassant was impressed with Schopenhauer's 'Metaphysics of Love' when he read it in Bourdeau's version; his bachelor-heroes in 'Le Verrou' (1882) regard Schopenhauer as their god: 'Ils citaient à tout instant Schopenhauer, leur dieu'.

However, Schopenhauer's influence on Maupassant went beyond the 'metaphysics of love'. Evidence of this comes in a ghoulish story, reminiscent of Hoffmann and Poe, written in the following year: 'Auprès d'un Mort' (1883). Here 'mon maître Schopenhauer' is described as '[le] philosophe allemand dont l'influence est désormais ineffaçable':

> Jouisseur désabusé, il a renversé les croyances, les espoirs, les poésies, les chimères, détruit les aspirations, ravagé la confiance des âmes, tué l'amour, abattu le culte idéal de la femme, crevé les illusions des coeurs, accompli la plus gigantesque besogne de sceptique qui ait jamais été faite. Il a tout traversé de sa moquerie, et tout vidé. Et aujourd'hui même, ceux qui l'exècrent semblent porter, malgré eux, en leurs esprits, des parcelles de sa pensée.

Maupassant shares Schopenhauer's pessimism and view of human suffering. In *Bel Ami* (1886) the old poet, Norbert de Varennes, is made to speak with Schopenhauer:

> Pourquoi souffrons-nous ainsi? C'est que nous étions nés sans doute pour vivre davantage selon la matière et moins selon l'esprit; mais, à force de penser, une disproportion s'est faite entre l'état de notre intelligence agrandie et les conditions immuables de notre vie.

Regardez les gens médiocres; à moins de grands désastres tombant sur eux ils se trouvent satisfaits, sans souffrir du malheur commun. Les bêtes non plus ne le sentent pas.

As Colin has pointed out, this passage derives from Bourdeau's *Pensées, maximes et fragments*.[11] Further echoes of Schopenhauer are found, too, in *Sur l'Eau* (1888) and 'L'Inutile Beauté' (1890). Passages such as these speak for themselves: 'Nous ne savons rien, nous ne voyons rien, nous ne pouvons rien, nous ne devinons rien, nous n'imaginons rien, nous sommes enfermés, emprisonnés en nous' (*Sur l'Eau*); 'Sais tu comment je conçois Dieu, dit-il: comme un monstrueux organe créateur inconnu de nous . . . Il crée parce que c'est sa fonction de Dieu; mais il est ignorant de ce qu'il fait' ('L'Inutile Beauté'; God is conceived in terms of the blind Schopenhauerian Will). It is therefore clear that Maupassant's 'Schopenhauerisme' was well established by the time that Moore met him in 1883.

One of the first, if not the first, of the *Médanistes* to take an interest in Schopenhauer was Henry Céard, whom Moore knew, although he was never very intimate with him.[12] As soon as Bourdeau's *Pensées, maximes et fragments* appeared in January 1880, Céard bought a copy, of which he wrote to Zola on 13 January 1880:

Contre l'habitude, la phrase est nette, acérée, incisive comme la phrase du XVIIIe siècle, spécialement celle de Chamfort. C'est moins spirituel que ce dernier, mais plus profond. Je vous prêterai cela quand vous serez à Paris. Peut-être y trouvez-vous matière à un article. Le système littéraire actuel a des points communs avec la doctrine de ce philosophe.[13]

For Céard the appeal of Schopenhauer was twofold: the fact that his philosophy, with its emphasis on pessimism and suffering, and its 'positivisme sceptique', touched 'le système littéraire actuel' at some important points, and the fact that 'jamais esprit ne fut plus foncièrement français'. These and other points are elaborated in a little-known but important article on Schopenhauer which appeared in *L'Express* on 8 August 1881. Céard writes there:

Schopenhauer est abominé par les professeurs de la philosophie officielle. D'autre part, les extraits de ses oeuvres qui viennent d'être édités se sont vendus à un nombre singulier d'éditions . . . jamais esprit ne fut plus foncièrement français; son mode de penser, son mode d'écrire n'ont rien de commun avec le génie germanique.

Schopenhauer a la phrase nette, courte, acérée, précise, au point que la traduction ne se sent point et qu'on croit lire en ses ouvrages l'ouvrage d'un auteur français. Cela possède la vivacité et le mordant de Chamfort. Du reste il parait l'avoir singulièrement pratiqué. Comme lui il excelle au tour piquant, au trait aigu, à l'épithète rare. Par lui, il se rattache à la grande école positiviste de la fin du XVIIIe siècle. Schopenhauer qu'on affecte de considérer comme le créateur d'un système continue tout simplement l'oeuvre de Diderot, Helvetius et d'Holbach. Seulement il montre plus d'autorité, ayant acquis plus de savoir. Ce n'est pas un philosophe spéculatif acculé dans l'empirisme, non, c'est un philosophe scientifique cherchant d'une façon certaine les moyens de rendre l'homme moins douloureux et la vie plus supportable . . . Sans enthousiasme, mais aussi sans colère, il contemple dans son effrayante mobilité le spectacle des erreurs terrestres.

> C'est un médecin, un expérimentateur, un physiologiste. Il sait les misères des fonctions, l'infériorité des organes, les faiblesses du cerveau, et ne leur demande par conséquent rien au delà de leur capacité et de leurs forces. Sa seule crainte est qu'on les surmène. Voilà justement en quoi me semble consister l'erreur répandue sur son compte. De ce qu'il acceptait les défaillances au même titre que les efforts, on a fait de lui un pessimiste. Par parti pris ou par ignorance, on a négligé de remarquer que s'il jugeait la vie sans gaieté, il ne la traitait jamais sans pitié.
>
> Jamais il ne s'irrite, jamais il ne dresse de réquisitoire. Les souffrances du monde l'attendrissent plus encore qu'elles ne le blessent, et s'il écrit ses livres, c'est moins dans le but de montrer son esprit et de faire valoir sa perspicacité en dévoilant des plaies insoupçonnées que dans l'intention plus pitoyable de procurer au lecteur désintéressé les moyens d'arriver à une somme moins considérable de tristesses . . .
>
> Pascal disait blâmer également 'et ceux qui prennent le parti de louer l'homme, et ceux qui le prennent de le divertir' et n'approuver que ceux qui *cherchent en gémissant*. Schopenhauer est bien ce philosophe attendri. C'est un pessimiste doux . . . Tirer parti de tout en vue de la diminution des souffrances, c'est le dernier mot de sa philosophie, la conclusion de toute son oeuvre. Il n'accuse pas la vie, il ne prêche ni la mélancolie ni le suicide, ce n'est ni un désespéré ni un railleur, c'est un organisateur, qui rêve pour l'humanité une adaptation si savante qu'aucun événement psychologique ne la trouverait au dépourvu, et qu'aucun accident moral ne deviendrait plus catastrophe.
>
> Par là, Schopenhauer séduit les esprits, il les console, il leur apporte le réconfort. Sa doctrine s'adresse à l'intelligence dans tout ce qu'elle a de supérieur, flatte l'homme dans tout ses instincts de liberté. Elle lui apprend que lui seul, tous les jours est l'artisan responsable devant lui seul du bonheur ou des malheurs de sa vie, et que son manque de savoir, l'obscurité de sa connaissance de lui–même constitue pour sa personne un danger immédiat, permanent. Elle est pratique, humaine, moderne, et voilà sans doute pourquoi, malgré la réprobation officielle de la Sorbonne, il s'est trouvé des acheteurs pour Schopenhauer et ses livres: hier on ne leur connaissait que des curieux, ils ont aujourd'hui des admirateurs et des fidèles.

Céard's own work (*Une belle journée*, 1881; *Terrains à vendre au bord de la mer*, 1906; etc.) is unimportant in our context, partly because his philosophy diverges from that of Schopenhauer, and partly because there is in any case no reason to suppose that Moore was any more interested in Céard's work than he was in the no less Schopenhauer-impregnated work of Rod (*Course à la mort*, 1885). We therefore return to Moore's early master, Zola.

While there is no proof positive that Céard did in fact lend Zola Jean Bourdeau's book, there is no reason to think that he did not do so; indeed, the evidence of *La Joie de Vivre* (1884) suggests that he almost certainly did so, for Zola's title came from it, as did his original alternative titles (La Vallée de Larmes; L'Espoir du Néant; Le Vieux Cynique; La Misère du Monde; Le Repos Sacré du Néant). On the face of it *La Joie de Vivre* was intended as a rejection of pessimism in favour of the 'joie de vivre' personified by Pauline Quenu, which Zola glossed as follows: 'La joie de vivre malgré les catastrophes; elle se relève et relève les autres. La bonté gaie, toujours gaie, dans le bonheur de l'habitude, dans l'espoir de l'habitude'.[14] Put thus, this sounds like a rejection of Schopenhauerian pessimism in favour of Nietzschean *Heiterkeit*. In fact, as Colin has shown, both Pauline Quenu and her symbolical opposite, Lazare Chanteau, were in part inspired by Schopenhauer's life and work. Zola's preparatory material for the novel included notes from both Bourdeau and Ribot. The Schopenhauer allusions in *La Joie de Vivre* are obvious enough. In Chapter III Pauline ponders Lazare's 'pessimisme mal digéré, dont il ne restait que . . . la grande poésie noire de Schopenhauer' and recalls Lazare referring, 'en plaisanteries froides', to 'les ruses de la Volonté qui mène le monde, la bêtise aveugle du vouloir-vivre.' She was repulsed by his argument that 'La vie était douleur, et il aboutissait . . . à la délivrance par l'anéantissement,' and would not allow herself to be beaten: 'elle envoyait carrément au diable son Schopenhauer, dont il avait voulu lui lire des passages; un homme qui écrivait un mal actroce des femmes!' Later in the same chapter she taunts Lazare: 'Ah! je ne t'ai pas dit! j'ai rêvé que ton Schopenhauer apprenait notre mariage dans l'autre monde, et qu'il revenait la nuit nous tirer par les pieds.' Her words put one in mind of Maupassant's 'Auprès d'un Mort' of 1883 and show the extent to which Schopenhauer had caught the popular imagination. In Chapter V Lazare is said to have retailed to Louise all Schopenhauer's views on women and love: 'Schopenhauer entier y passait, avec ses brutalités, dont la jeune fille, rougissante, s'égayait beaucoup.' Lazare sinks deeper and deeper into 'la haine furieuse de l'existence': 'Aussi renchérissait-il encore sur les théories du "vieux", comme il nommait Schopenhauer, dont il récitait de mémoire les passages violents. Il parlait de tuer la volonté de vivre, pour faire cesser cette parade barbare et imbécile de la vie, que la force maîtresse du monde se donne en spectacle, dans un but d'égoïsme inconnu.' At the end of the novel Pauline, of whom Huysmans said 'c'est Pauline qui est la vraie schopenhaueriste', declares that Lazare 'l'avait convertie au grand saint Schopenhauer, qu'elle voulait rester fille afin de travailler à la délivrance universelle.'

Colin is surely right to argue that Zola's wretched Schopenhauerian pessimist, Lazare, is 'un de ces "schopenhauristes" dont parle la grande presse, plutôt qu'un véritable disciple de Schopenhauer',[15] for this is in line with Zola's own reply to a letter from E. Rod concerning the 'Schopenhauerism' of Lazare. Zola wrote there: 'Jamais de ma vie je n'ai voulu en faire un métaphysicien, un parfait disciple de Schopenhauer, car cette espèce n'existe pas en France. Je dis au contraire que Lazare a mal digéré la doctrine, qu'il est un produit des idées pessimistes telles qu'elles circulent chez nous.'[16] There is therefore no reason to doubt the truth of T.G. West's conclusion: 'As far as Schopenhauer is concerned, Lazare is not used as the philosophic *porte-parole* of his creator, . . . but is the embodiment of a misdirected type of pessimist nourished on "Schopenhauerisme mal digéré".'[17]

What is more important from our point of view is the fact that Lazare may well have provided Moore with his initial model for the abominable Mike Fletcher, himself very much a *Schopenhaueriste* of the Parisian press and salons. *La Joie de Vivre* may have been intended as an attack on pessimism; but for George Moore it could well have been (particularly if he read it shortly after publication) a further source not so much of Schopenhauerian ideas, as of the idea that references to Schopenhauer were *de rigueur* in the contemporary novel. Following the appearance of *La Joie de Vivre*, J.-K. Huysmans wrote to Zola, in March 1884, in an attempt to convert Zola to his own adherence to Schopenhauer's philosophy:

> Je trouve dans ce livre une note que vous avez bien frôlée, à certaines parties, déjà, mais que vous n'aviez jamais donnée, entière, complète, avec un accent aussi particulier: une note de tendresse douloureuse. Toute la partie, après la mort de Mme Chanteau, est à ce point de vue typiquement superbe. Et la mort du chien, avec le retour des idées navrantes, est une des belles pages que vous ayez écrites et une page à part dans tout ce que vous avez fait. L'accouchement est terrible et d'une simplicité qui m'étonne car c'est là le rêve! Pauline est bien dévidée, mais peut-être un peu bien angéliquement séraphique, d'âme, dans sa grosse chair. L'esprit de sacrifice dont elle est animée peut évidemment se produire, mais c'est égal, la petite fille du Ventre de Paris est devenue singulièrement céleste. Quant à Lazare, je le trouve étudié, au point de vue psychologique, de main de maître — mais il y a là une théorie du schopenhauerisme qui ne me semble pas parfaitement exacte. Tout le côté absolument consolant de cette doctrine est anti-romantique, anti-wertheriste, bien que vous en puissiez dire, n'y est pas assez, je trouve, exposé. — Songez que c'est la théorie de la résignation, la même théorie absolument que celle de l'*Imitation de Jésus-Christ*, moins la panacée future, remplacée par l'esprit de patience, par le parti pris de tout accepter sans se plaindre, par l'attente bienfaisante de la mort, considérée, ainsi que la religion, comme une délivrance et non comme une peur. Je sais bien que vous ne croyez pas au pessimisme et que la préface de Bourdeau aux *Pensées* de Schopenhauer déclare que cet homme prodigieux avait la crainte de la mort — mais, la théorie est plus haute, passe au-dessus de l'homme qui n'appliquait pas à lui-même ses idées, mais, dans l'impossibilité où les gens intelligents se trouvent de croire au catholicisme, ces idées sont, à coup sûr, les plus consolantes, les plus logiques, les plus évidentes qui puissent être. Au fond, si l'on n'est pas pessimiste, il n'y a qu'à être chrétien ou anarchiste; un des trois pour peu qu'on y réfléchisse.
>
> Mais tout ça est en dehors de la question. La vérité est que vous avez donné une note spéciale, non seulement dans les *Rougon-Macquart*, mais dans le livre actuel — un arrachement doux, un renonciation mélancolique. Au fond, c'est Pauline qui est la vraie schopenhaueriste, comme vous l'avez laissé entendre, en riant — mais c'est vrai![18]

Confirmation of the truth of Huysmans' remark that 'c'est Pauline qui est la vraie schopenhaueriste' comes from Zola's own notes for the novel, where we read: 'Pauline, c'est elle qui est avec Schopenhauer pour son renoncement, pour sa stérilité voulue . . . pour son altruisme, mais elle ne pousse pas jusqu'a la négation de la vie'.[19]

The more important point here, however, concerns Huysmans himself, for when all is said and done, Zola was the least enthusiastic about Schopenhauer of all the *Médanistes*. Moore knew and admired Huysmans' work, and by this time might well already have discovered the Schopenhauerian ideas in Huysmans' *A Vau l'Eau* (1882) or — less likely — in *En Ménage* (1881). In an unpublished letter to Théo Hannon dated 29 March 1881, Huysmans quoted the reviewer in the *National* as saying of *En Ménage* 'c'est le scepticisme et le schopenhauerisme [sic]', and commented 'ça c'est moins bête!'[20] However, while this makes it likely that Huysmans read Bourdeau's selection shortly after its publication in 1880, the fact that Schopenhauer is not mentioned by name in *En Ménage* makes it unlikely that Moore will have associated the novel with Schopenhauerian ideas. It is not even known that he read it. With *A Vau l'Eau* it is rather a different matter, for although the story as a whole puts one in mind of George Gissing rather than George Moore, its wretched hero, Folantin, could have provided Moore with a model for Mike Fletcher. As he makes his way home at the end of the work Folantin recalls Schopenhauer's statement in the Fourth Book of *The World as Will and Idea* ('The Assertion and Denial of the Will'), quoted by Bourdeau, that 'la vie de l'homme oscille comme un pendule entre la douleur et l'ennui'. It is scarcely an exaggeration to say that Folantin 'gives himself up totally to a Schopenhauerian pessimism'.[21] Huysmans' biographer has written:

> authority for [Huysmans'] pessimistic beliefs was provided by Schopenhauer's *Aphorisms*, which caused a sensation in intellectual circles when they were first translated into French in 1880. Huysmans discovered that they reflected many of his own most cherished ideas — that life was futile and unpleasant, that woman was fundamentally ignoble, that suffering was a sign of superiority, and so on — and it is not surprising that he gave unhesitating adherence to Schopenhauer's philosophy.[22]

Thus it is also not surprising that *A Vau l'Eau* is 'impregnated with the ideas of that period's favourite philosopher, Arthur Schopenhauer'.[23] Now while there is no evidence that Moore's Mike Fletcher, wretched protagonist of the novel of that name, is modelled on Folantin, there can be no doubt that he belongs together with Zola's Lazare, and with Huysmans' Folantin and Des Esseintes. Moore's great enthusiasm for *A Rebours* (1884) probably derives from his knowledge of *A Vau l'Eau*, of which it was intended to be an extension. This brings us to *A Rebours*, for if Folantin ends by quoting Schopenhauer with approval, his more interesting successor, Des Esseintes, goes further in regarding Schopenhauer's philosophy as 'la grande consolatrice . . . des âmes élevées'.

When Moore first met Huysmans, is not known, although it may well have been while he was living in Paris in the 1870s; be this as it may, both men were certainly present at the house-warming party at the new offices of the *Revue Indépendante* in the Rue de la Chaussée d'Antin on 26 November 1887, the rhyming invitation to which was written by Mallarmé. By this time *A Rebours* had appeared and had been first reviewed and then copied by Moore. It created a sensation on its appearance in 1884. George Moore reviewed it in the *Pall Mall Gazette* for 2 September 1884 with, in Hone's judicious phrase, 'as much enthusiasm as the editor would allow',[24] signalling his personal interest in this 'curious book' by pronouncing it to be 'so exotic it was fit only for the literary gourmet'. Later, in the *Confessions*, he was to refer to *A Rebours* as 'a prodigious book': 'A page of Huysmans is as a dose of opium, a glass of something exquisite and spiritous . . . Huysmans goes to my soul like a gold ornament of Byzantine workmanship: there is in his style the yearning charm of arches, a sense of ritual, the passion of the Gothic, of the window.' Moore's admiration for the Decadent masterpiece was so great that he fashioned his *Confessions* as its English equivalent. It may have been Huysmans, too, who taught Moore to put aesthetics before ethics, form before ideas: 'Huysmans is quite right, ideas are well enough until you are twenty, afterwards only words are bearable' (*Confessions*). The fruits of Moore's enthusiasm were soon seen: Téodor de Wyzewa, writing in *La Revue Indépendante* in September 1887, found it necessary to deny that John Norton, hero of Moore's *A Mere Accident* (1887) was a copy of Des Esseintes, although he did argue that *A Mere Accident* was about 'la guérison de Des Esseintes'.[25] Later scholars have been in no doubt about Moore's indebtedness to Huysmans. M. Steward, writing in 1934, described John Norton as 'a pale carbon copy of Des Esseintes, a beef-tea aesthete',[26] while Huysmans' biographer, Robert Baldick, described *A Mere Accident* as being (together with *Mike Fletcher*) 'manifestly inspired' by *A Rebours*;[27] John Norton, in *A Mere Accident* and *Mike Fletcher*, copies Des Esseintes in his furnishing schemes, his reading of Schopenhauer, his taste in church music.[28] Nor is this all, for there remains the matter of Christian Latinity. Whether it is true that Moore spent summer 1886 reading 'all the Latin authors of the Middle Ages from the second to the eighth century' for a chapter of *A Mere Accident*, as he claimed to have done,[29] is doubtful; the characteristic odour of hyperbole is unmistakable. What is certain is that Moore's chapter exactly parallels Chapter III of *A Rebours*, which was clearly his inspiration. More recently G.A. Cevasco has argued that George Moore was so impressed by *A Rebours*, 'that soon, consciously and unconsciously, he began to imitate its style and borrow its themes':[30] the hero of *A Mere Accident* is modelled on Des Esseintes, Moore saw his *Confessions* as the English equivalent of *A Rebours*, and *Mike Fletcher* too was inspired (if that is the word) by Huysmans' novel.

Moore's indebtedness to *A Rebours* is beyond question. What concerns us now, however, is Huysmans' own interest in Schopenhauer, which could have rubbed off on Moore via *A Rebours*. In 1884, in the letter to Zola which I have already quoted, Huysmans wrote that Schopenhauer's ideas remain 'les plus consolantes, les plus logiques, les plus évidentes qui puissent être.'

By this time, however, Huysmans' Schopenhauerism was on the wane; it is not for nothing that Des Esseintes finally abjures his pessimism, albeit only after that famous passage in which he links Schopenhauer's virulently anti-Christian doctrine of resignation with the *Imitatio Christi.* His starting-point is his vision of the Church proclaiming to mankind the horror of life, the malignity of fate:

Peu à peu enfin, ces arguties s'évanouirent. Il vit, en quelque sorte, du haut de son esprit, le panorama de l'Eglise, son influence héréditaire sur l'humanité, depuis des siècles; il se la représenta, désolée et grandiose, énonçant à l'homme l'horreur de la vie, l'inclémence de la destinée; prêchant la patience, la contrition, l'esprit de sacrifice; tâchant de panser les plaies, en montrant les blessures saignantes du Christ; assurant des privilèges divins, promettant la meilleure part du paradis aux affligés; exhortant la créature humaine à souffrir, à présenter à Dieu comme un holocauste ses tribulations et ses offenses, ses vicissitudes et ses peines. Elle devenait véritablement éloquente, maternelle aux misérables, pitoyable aux opprimés, menaçante pour les oppresseurs et les despotes.

Ici, Des Esseintes reprenait pied. Certes, il était satisfait de cet aveu de l'ordure sociale, mais alors, il se révoltait contre le vague remède d'une espérance en une autre vie. Schopenhauer était plus exact; sa doctrine et celle de l'Eglise partaient d'un point de vue commun; lui aussi se basait sur l'iniquité et sur la turpitude du monde, lui aussi jetait, avec l'*Imitation de Notre-Seigneur*, cette clameur douloureuse: 'C'est vraiment une misère que de vivre sur la terre!' Lui aussi prêchait le néant de l'existence, les avantages de la solitude, avisait l'humanité que quoi qu'elle fit, de quelque côté qu'elle se tournât, elle demeurerait malheureuse: pauvre, à cause des souffrances qui naissent des privations; riche, en raison de l'invincible ennui qu'engendre l'abondance; mais il ne vous prônait aucune panacée, ne vous berçait, pour remédier à d'inévitables maux, par aucun leurre.

Il ne vous soutenait pas le révoltant système du péché originel; ne tentait point de vous prouver que celui-là est un Dieu souverainement bon qui protège les chenapans, aide les imbéciles, ècrase l'enfance, abêtit la vieillesse, châtie les incoupables; il n'exaltait pas les bienfaits d'une Providence qui a inventé cette abomination, inutile, incompréhensible, injuste, inepte, la souffrance physique; loin de s'essayer à justifier, ainsi que l'Eglise, la nécessité des tourments et des épreuves, il s'écriait, dans sa miséricorde indignée: 'Si un Dieu a fait ce monde, je n'aimerais pas à être ce Dieu; la misère du monde me déchirerait le coeur.'

Ah! lui seul était dans le vrai! qu'étaient toutes les pharmacopées évangéliques à côté de ses traités d'hygiène spirituelle? Il ne prétendait rien guérir, n'offrait aux malades aucune compensation, aucun espoir: mais sa théorie du Pessimisme était, en somme, la grande consolatrice des intelligences choisies, des âmes élevées; elle révélait la société telle qu'elle est, insistait sur la sottise innée des femmes, vous signalait les ornières, vous sauvait des désillusions en vous avertissant de restreindre autant que possible vos espérances, de n'en point du tout concevoir, si vous vous en sentiez la force, de vous estimer enfin heureux si, à des moments inopinés, il ne vous dégringolait pas sur la tête de formidables tuiles.

Elancée de la même piste que l'*Imitation*, cette théorie aboutissait, elle aussi, mais sans s'égarer parmi de mystérieux dédales et d'invraisemblables routes, au même endroit, à la résignation, au laisser-faire.

Seulement, si cette résignation tout bonnement issue de la constatation d'un état de choses déplorable et de l'impossibilité d'y rien changer, était accessible aux riches de l'esprit, elle n'était que plus difficilement saisissable aux pauvres dont la bienfaisante religion calmait plus aisément alors les revendications et les colères.

Ces réflexions soulageaient Des Esseintes d'un lourd poids; les aphorismes du grand Allemand apaisaient le frisson de ses pensées et cependant, les points de contact des ces deux doctrines les aidaient à se rappeler mutuellement à la mémoire . . .

(*A Rebours*, Chapter VII)

The only surprising thing about this passage is the fact that it has surprised the critics, for Huysmans is only making a parallel that Schopenhauer himself makes, although the philosopher — who regarded himself as a Christian philosopher *par excellence* — does not happen to choose the *Imitatio Christi* as one of his examples of Christian mysticism. This is a point to which we shall return in connexion with *The Brook Kerith.*

By 1891 Huysmans had recanted; in a letter dated 29 April 1891 he wrote to Jules Destrée: 'Quand je songe que dans *A Rebours*, j'ai à peu près mis Schopenhauer au-dessus de l'*Imitation.* Faut-il être bête!'[31] Shortly afterwards in November of the same year, he wrote in another letter: 'Jadis, j'ai beaucoup aimé Schopenhauer — aujourd'hui il me désenchante. J'apprécie encore l'exactitude de ses constats, mais le néant de ses conclusions me gêne. Dans l'intelligible abomination qu'est la vie, il ne peut pas ne rien y avoir.'[32] He came back to the same point, first in *En Route* (1895), and then in the Preface to a new edition of *A Rebours* in 1903. In *En Route* he wrote:

plus nettement que Schopenhauer, l'Eglise déclarait qu'il n'y avait rien à souhaiter, ici-bas, rien à attendre; mais là où s'arrêtaient les procès-verbaux du philosophe, elle, continuait, franchissait les limites des sens, divulguait le but, précisait les fins.

Puis, se disait-il, tout bien considéré, l'argument de Schopenhauer tant prôné contre le Créateur et tiré de la misère et de l'injustice du monde, n'est pas, quand on y réfléchit, irrésistible, car le monde n'est pas ce que Dieu l'a fait, mais bien ce que l'homme en a fait.

His fullest statement on the subject was made, however, in the 'Preface écrite vingt ans après le roman' of 1903:

Je pourrais très bien signer maintenant les pages d'*A rebours* sur l'Eglise, car elles paraissent avoir été, en effet, écrites par un catholique.

Je me croyais loin de la religion pourtant! Je ne songeais pas que, de Schopenhauer que j'admirais plus que de raison, à l'Ecclésiaste et au Livre de Job, il n'y avait qu'un pas. Les prémisses sur le Pessimisme sont les mêmes, seulement, lorsqu'il s'agit de conclure, le philosophe se dérobe. J'aimais ses idées sur l'horreur de la vie, sur la bêtise du monde, sur l'inclémence de la destinée; je les aime également dans les Livres saints; mais les observations de Schopenhauer n'aboutissent à rien; il vous laisse, pour ainsi parler, en plan; ses aphorismes ne sont, en somme, qu'un herbier de plaintes sèches; l'Église, elle, explique les origines et les causes, signale les fins, présente les remèdes; elle ne se contente pas de vous donner une consultation d'âme, elle vous traite et elle vous guérit, alors que le médicastre allemand, après vous avoir bien démontré que l'affection dont vous souffrez est incurable, vous tourne, en ricanant, le dos.

Son Pessimisme n'est autre que celui des Ecritures auxquelles il l'a emprunté. Il n'a pas dit plus que Salomon, plus que Job, plus même que l'*Imitation* qui a résumé, bien avant lui, toute sa philosophie en une phrase: 'C'est vraiment une misère que de vivre sur la terre!'

A distance, ces similitudes et ces dissemblances s'avèrent nettement, mais à cette époque, si je les percevais, je ne m'y attardais point; le besoin de conclure ne me tentait pas; la route tracée par Schopenhauer était carrossable et d'aspect varié, je m'y promenais tranquillement, sans désir d'en connaître le bout; en ce temps-là, je n'avais aucune clarté réelle sur les échéances, aucune appréhension des dénouements; les mystères du catéchisme me paraissaient enfantins; comme tous les catholiques, du reste, j'ignorais parfaitement ma religion; je ne me rendais pas compte que tout est mystère, que nous ne vivons que dans le mystère, que si le hasard existait, il serait encore plus mystérieux que la Providence. Je n'admettais pas la douleur infligée par un Dieu, je m'imaginais que le Pessimisme pouvait être le consolateur des âmes élevées. Quelle bêtise! c'est cela qui était peu expérimental, peu document humain, pour me servir d'un terme cher au naturalisme. Jamais le Pessimisme n'a consolé et les malades de corps et les alités d'âme!

Je souris, alors qu'après tant d'années je relis les pages où ces théories, si résolument fausses, sont affirmées.

No doubts Colin's conclusion is right: 'Schopenhauer n'a été pour Huysmans que le compagnon de route d'un moment'.[33]

It is the fact that that moment produced *A Rebours* that makes it so important in this context. Huysmans does not only develop his argument in *A Rebours* by means of a parallel between Schopenhauer's ideas and those of the Church; he rejects the latter in favour of the former — the words 'Si un Dieu a fait ce monde, je n'aimerais pas à être ce Dieu; la misère du monde me déchirerait le coeur' (Chapter VII) come straight from Bourdeau. And Schopenhauer's pessimism was seen as 'la grande consolatrice des intelligences choisies, des âmes élevées' (ibid.). This is an idea which George Moore could not possibly have resisted; and all the evidence suggests that he did not want to resist it. After all, it has been plausibly argued that John Norton, Edward Dayne and Mike Fletcher are all based on Des Esseintes. And they are all *Schopenhaueristes*.

It will, then, be readily agreed that Rémy de Gourmont was fully justified in writing that 'Notre éducation philosophique, à quelques-uns, avait . . . été faite par le "Schopenhauer" de M. Bourdeau et celui de M. Ribot.' It is true that the Naturalists and Decadents did not have any very profound knowledge of Schopenhauer's ideas, or make very profound use of them, but their 'symbolic . . . use of his name as a shibboleth or rallying cry'[34] must have attracted Moore's attention, for he shared their pessimism; if Schopenhauer 'flattered their nascent despair with the hint of a sophisticated metaphysic',[35] this is precisely what he was also to do for George Moore.

Moore will first have heard of Schopenhauer in Paris in the 1870s, and on his visits to Paris in the early 1880s he must have been impressed by the extent to which Schopenhauer was appearing in the French novel, which he took as his model. Schopenhauer features in the French novel of the early 1880s in much the same kind of way as in Moore's own novels of the later 1880s. The influence of novels such as Zola's *La Joie de Vivre* and Huysmans' *A Vau l'Eau* and *A Rebours* is unmistakable; here are the models for *A Mere Accident*, *Mike Fletcher* and *Confessions*.

But if Moore's interest in Schopenhauer obviously came from Paris, his actual knowledge of Schopenhauer and his more specific echoes come, mostly, from *The World as Will and Idea*, Haldane and Kemp's translation of which appeared in 1883–86. The first French version, *Le Monde comme Volonté et comme Représentation* (tr. Cantacuzène), appeared in 1886. In practical terms his *knowledge* of Schopenhauer is therefore likely to date from not earlier than 1883. It is true that there were two earlier translations of works by Schopenhauer into English, but the works in question (*The Will in Nature*, tr. P. Eckler, New York, 1877; *Select Essays*, tr. G. Droppers & C.A.P. Dachsel, Milwaukee, 1881) attracted so little attention that Moore is most unlikely even to have heard of them; certainly there is no evidence that he did.

The evidence (in the form of a comparison of apparent echoes of Schopenhauer in Moore's works of the years 1887–1889 with the text of the English translation of *The World as Will and Idea*) strongly suggests that by 1886 Moore had read some or all of the important Fourth Book ('The Assertion and Denial of the Will to Live')[36] of the Haldane-Kemp translation, and may also have looked into some of the Supplements to the Fourth Book.[37] It is particularly interesting that these are the same sections of Schopenhauer's work which George Gissing used so much more effectively in *his* 1889 novel *The Nether World*. The evidence of *Mike Fletcher* in particular suggests that Moore was, as usual, able to obtain a relatively sound (if superficial) impression with a minimum of actual reading. Indeed, only about half of the various allusions and apparent allusions to Schopenhauer in his work of the years 1887–1889 seem to be based on an actual reading of the philosopher; the others are couched in such vague, fuzzy terms that one is sometimes left wondering whether he has understood the philosopher, or is merely repeating something he has heard in conversation. While Moore may well have first heard of Schopenhauer from Alexis or Céard in the early 1880s, it will have been his reading of *A Rebours* in September 1884 that first drew his attention to Schopenhauer; but it was probably conversations with Edouard Dujardin, in 1886–87, that kindled his curiosity into the headlong enthusiasm which immediately proceeded, in his novels of the late 1880s, to go too far. The timing is exactly right, and he is not known to have had a Schopenhauer-enthusiast among his close friends until he met Dujardin; later on, of course, he had several, including W.B. Yeats, who wrote to Sturge Moore in December 1927: 'Schopenhauer can do no wrong in my eyes. I no more quarrel with his errors than I do with a mountain cataract. Error is but the abyss into which he precipitates his truth.'[38] Moore corresponded with Dujardin from November 1886 onwards, and *Confessions* was serialized in Dujardin's *Revue Indépendante* in 1888. In *Ave* Moore related how he and Dujardin used to discuss Schopenhauer and Nietzsche at length. The evidence of Moore's most Schopenhauerian novel, *Mike Fletcher* (1889) suggests that he may well have been carried away by Dujardin's enthusiasm.

At some stage Téodor de Wyzewa, the earliest French Nietzsche-enthusiast and prolific writer on Wagner, will have been involved in these discussions, for Dujardin shared a flat with Wyzewa, at which Moore often stayed. It was in 1887 that Moore got to know Wyzewa, who reviewed *A Mere Accident* in the *Revue Indépendante*; no doubt Wyzewa's article on Nietzsche in *La Revue Politique et Littéraire* in 1891 was one of the things that prompted Moore to take an interest in Nietzsche. Later he enthused over Daniel Halévy's *La vie de Frédéric Nietzsche* (1909), for he knew Halévy well, having been intro- duced to his father by Dégas, and was a neighbour of his in the Rue de la Tour des Dames in the late 1880s. Nietzsche was to be Moore's next 'fad' after Schopenhauer. More to the point at present, however, is the fact that Moore could also have discussed Schopenhauer with Halévy. In his life of Nietzsche Halévy included a striking summary of Schopenhauer's philosophy, which put the emphasis on what had by then influenced Moore's novels of the later 1880s, the 'Will':

> Le monde que décrit Schopenhauer est redoutable. Aucune Providence ne l'oriente, aucun Dieu ne l'habite, des lois inflexibles l'enchaînent à travers le temps et l'espace; mais son essence éternelle est indifférente aux lois, étrangère à la raison: c'est l'aveugle Volonté qui nous presse dans la vie. Tous les phénomènes de l'univers sont les rayonnements de cette Volonté, de même que tous les jours des ans rayonnent d'un même soleil. Elle est invariable, elle est infinie: divisée, resserrée dans l'espace, 'elle se nourrit d'elle- même, puisque, hors d'elle il n'y a rien, et qu'elle est une volonté affamée'. Donc, elle se déchire et souffre. La vie est un désir, le désir est un tourment sans fin. Les bonnes âmes du XIXe siècle croient à la dignité de l'homme, au Progrès. Une superstition les dupe. La Volonté ignore les hommes, 'derniers venus sur la Terrre et qui vivent en moyenne trente ans'. Le Progrès est la sotte invention des philosophes inspirés par les foules: la Volonté, scandale pour la raison, n'a point d'origine, point de fin; elle est absurde, et l'univers qu'elle anime n'a pas de sens . . .[39]

II. George Moore, *Schopenhaueriste*

At this stage let us leave Paris with Moore in 1800 in order to consider the work that he proceeded to produce, while at the same time remembering that he was a frequent visitor to Paris in the early 1880s, when the Schopenhauer fashion was at its height there. Since the novel with the title reminiscent of contemporary Parisian melodrama, *Aristocracy of Vice*, on which Moore told his mother he was working in winter 1878–79, was abandoned, it is the *Pagan Poems* of 1881 that pose the first problem. It has been claimed[40] that the following lines from the long 'Ode to a Beggar Girl' derive from Schopenhauer:

> 'Life,' you say, 'is hard to bear'.
> Every day it will grow harder,
> Pluck up courage and escape
> All this misery and woe;
> Death is always kindly — die!

However, while these lines reflect the pessimism which Moore had clearly concluded to be *de rigueur*, there is not the slightest need for them to have anything to do with Schopenhauer, even if they do remind one of what Oscar Wilde, in a letter to William Ward dated 26 July 1876 quoted his mother as saying:

> Her [Lady Wilde's] last pessimist, Schopenhauer, says the whole human race ought on a given day, after a strong remonstrance *firmly but respectfully* urged on by God, to walk into the sea and leave the world tenantless, but of course some skulking wretches would hide and be left behind to people the world again I am afraid.[41]

Moore knew the Wildes, who lived not far from the Moores during George's and Oscar's boyhood, but by 1876 he was unfortunately in Paris and so presumably missed hearing an amusing early account of Schopenhauer.

Moore's first published novel, *A Modern Lover* (1883), begins with the despair to the point of suicide which his knowledge of Schopenhauer *later* allowed him to orchestrate.[42] At this stage, I think, the theme will have owed nothing whatsoever to Schopenhauer, but is variously typical of the 1880s and of the melodramatically inclined young Moore. Besides, as Moore himself reminds us, 'pessimism . . . is as old as the world' (*Conversations in Ebury Street*, Ebury Edition, 1936, 76). Those who see 'Schopenhauerian' ideas in his early poems should, I think, remember his words. But if there is nothing of Schopenhauer in *A Modern Lover*, the main motifs that are associated with Schopenhauer in the novels of

1887–1889 (despair; suicide; fate; illusions; the connexion between love and death; etc.) *are* there, as is the 'veil'-metaphor, of which Moore was already fond before he discovered the 'veil of Maya'. Harding, the 'cynical atheist' of *Mike Fletcher* (1889), first appears in *A Modern Lover* as 'Harding, the novelist, whose books were vigorously denounced by the press, as being both immoral and cynical'; but it is only in *Mike Fletcher* that this Moore-like figure is made to speak with Schopenhauer. *A Modern Lover* confirms, then, that in 1883 Moore did not know Schopenhauer's work. Nor is there any sign of Schopenhauer in his next novel, *A Mummer's Wife* (1885).

The first book by Moore in which Schopenhauer is named is *A Drama in Muslin* (1886). There are two such references. In the first Moore alludes to 'the calm will-less knowledge that Schopenhauer holds up to us as the highest ideal to be attained' (Book II, Chapter 3: 166). This is an echo of the 'pure, will-less knowledge' of which Schopenhauer speaks in the essay 'On the Pure Subject of Knowledge' (*WWI*, III, 127) and which he describes in 'The Assertion and Denial of the Will' (ibid., I, 504f). When Moore uses the word 'will-less', this is its source. In the second passage he links Wordsworth and Schopenhauer:

> the sensitivity of some [individuals] is so great that they anticipate . . . ideas not yet in existence, but which are quickening in the womb of the world. Wordsworth is an example of this foreseeing, forefeeling, forehearing. For at the time of writing the 'Excursion', the influence of the German pessimists had not penetrated into England; Schopenhauer was an unknown name; and yet poet and philosopher seem but the expansion of a single mind.
>
> Is it therefore unnatural or even extraordinary that Alice Barton, who is if anything a representative woman of 1885, should have . . . divined the doctrines of Eduard von Hartmann, the entire and unconditional resignation of personal existence into the arms of the cosmic process? Cecilia . . . with her black hatred of life concentrated upon a loathing of the origin of existence, was but another manifestation of the same stratum of thought. (Book III, Chapter 1: 228f).

A few years later, in an article on 'Some of Balzac's Minor Pieces' in *The Fortnightly Review* for October 1889, Moore similarly wrote of a 'mysterious instinctive comprehension of Schopenhauer's philosophy' being contained in the last pages of Balzac's *Le Lys dans la Vallée*, concluding from this that Balzac was very much in advance of his time. So far as Wordsworth is concerned, Moore is no doubt thinking of the passage in *The Excursion*, Book IV ('The Voice of the Universe') where Wordsworth describes how man, through something very like the 'calm will-less knowledge' of which Moore speaks, may overcome the need to bewail the burden of existence.

A second reference to Eduard von Hartmann in the third (1889) edition of the *Confessions of a Young Man* (344) names the source of the 'doctrines of Eduard von Hartman [sic]' which Alice Barton is said to have 'divined'. This doctrine, 'the entire and unconditional resignation of personal existence into the arms of the cosmic process' (*A Drama in Muslin*, 229), is a paraphrase of Hartmann's ideal, 'the complete devotion of the personality to the world process' (*Philosophy of the Unconscious*, tr. W.C. Coupland, 1931, III, 133). The ideas which she expresses and which are linked with Hartmann are also taken, more or less verbatim, from the same source. She argues that 'the ideal should . . . lie in reconciliation — no, reconciliation is not the word I want; I scarcely know how to express myself — well, in making the two ends meet — in making the ends of nature the ends also of what we call our conscience.' (*A Drama in Muslin*, 228). Her hesitant words come straight from Hartmann, who writes that 'a practical philisophy . . . [can] contain . . . only the full RECONCILIATION with life' (*Philosophy of the Unconscious*, III, 134) having previously argued that 'the principle of practical philosophy consists in this, TO MAKE THE ENDS OF THE UNCONSCIOUS ENDS OF OUR OWN CONSCIOUSNESS' (ibid; III, 133). Moore's later criticism of Schopenhauer's remarks on the subject of suicide as 'feeble and ineffective' presumably comes from the same source (ibid., III, 100f). It is therefore clear that Moore read the *Philosophy of the Unconscious* shortly after Coupland's translation first appeared in 1884. Whether he also knew *The Religion of the Future* (tr. E. Dare), which appeared in 1886, the same year as *A Drama in Muslin*, I do not know. Despite these two echoes there is no reason whatsoever to suppose that he, unlike Thomas Hardy, was seriously interested in Hartmann's philosophy; indeed, the evidence collected here suggests that he could not possibly have been. It is, I think, safe to conclude from the later allusion to the *Philosophy of the Unconscious* in the third (1889) edition of the *Confessions* (344) that he himself regarded Hartmann's philosophy as a 'silly vulgarisation' of the more aesthetic philosophy of Schopenhauer.

One could argue that these references to Schopenhauer and Hartmann in *A Drama in Muslin* amount to little more than authorial name-dropping, or, as Noël puts it: 'C'est vraisemblablement le désir de représenter objectivement l'esprit du temps qui amène ces deux noms sous sa plume'.[43] 'In the eighties', Moore was to write later, 'it seemed enough to flaunt ideas on all subjects.' In the context (*Conversations in Ebury Street*, Chapter 4; Ebury Edition, 1936, 61) this signals Moore's new preoccupation as a writer: his desire to vie with Landor and display his critical ideas in the form of conversations. More generally the remark applies to Schopenhauer, and also to Nietzsche, so far as George Moore is concerned. It is a peculiarly Moorish remark, for although the 1880s marked the beginning of a period of intellectual adventure that lasted until 1914, it could be argued that few serious writers were content to 'flaunt' ideas in quite the way that Moore did. Hardy and Gissing certainly were not. No doubt this is why Susan

Mitchell chose to stigmatize Moore as 'a born literary bandit'.[44] *A Drama in Muslin* confirms that Moore had registered Schopenhauer's name by 1885, when it was written; but it also shows that at that time he had no first-hand knowledge of Schopenhauer's work; if he had already read *The World as Will and Idea*, his rendering of Alice Barton's despair would have reflected the fact. Alice's and Cecilia's attitudes to life do, however, show that he had read Hartmann's *Philosophy of the Unconscious* (tr. W.C. Coupland, 3 vols., 1884). He may have been led to Hartmann by F. Bowen's *Modern Philosophy* (1877), and it may in turn have been his reading of Hartmann that prompted him to get down to reading Schopenhauer.

The first book by Moore to reveal some knowledge of Schopenhauer's work is *A Mere Accident* (1887), a psychical investigation of bachelorhood which immediately puts one in mind of Schopenhauer's life. The main character of the novel, John Norton, based on Moore's cousin Edward Martyn, reappears in *Spring Days* (1888), *Mike Fletcher* (1889) and *Celibates* (1895). A Catholic ascete, John Norton is torn between the spirit and the world; after losing his love, Kitty Hare, he finally resolves that the world will be his monastery. It is when Moore is introducing his troubled ascetic hero that an apparent echo of *The World as Will and Idea* is heard:

> before . . . picking up the thread of the story, which will of course be no more than an experimental demonstration of the working of the brain into which we are looking, we must take note of two curious mental traits both living side by side . . . : an intense and ever pulsatory horror of death, a sullen contempt and often a ferocious hatred of life. The stress of mind engendered by the alternating of these themes of suffering would have rendered life an unbearable burden to John, had he not found anchorage in an invincible belief in God . . . (28)

If it were not for the fact that Moore names Schopenhauer later in the book, there would be no occasion here to think of the German philosopher at all. But since Schopenhauer *is* named, it seems very likely that the 'unbearable burden' of life comes from the Fourth Book of *The World as Will and Idea*, the subject of which ('The Assertion and Denial of the Will to Live') is precisely John Norton's dilemma. Schopenhauer writes there of how life can be 'an unbearable burden' to man (*WWI*, I, 402). We shall see presently that this was the section of Schopenhauer's work that Moore knew best, and that he was sufficiently impressed by the passage for 'unbearable' and 'burden' to become favourite words of his for a time.[45]

John Norton's 'intense depression of the spirits' wears a Schopenhauerian aspect when he lies contemplating 'the poor worm that writhed out its life in view of the pitiless stars' and 'longing with a fierce wild longing to shake off the burning garment of consciousness' (30).

The fact that he has occasionally 'moaned and shrieked with . . . horror of death and a worse horror of life' (56) shows him struggling in the toils of the Will to Live. When, later in the novel, Moore describes the 'manifestation of modern pessimism' in John Norton, he does so with specific reference to Schopenhauer:

> His happiness and ambitions appeared to him less than the scattering of a little sand on the sea-shore. Joy is passion, passion is suffering . . . when we attain the object of our desire, we must perforce neglect it in favour of something still unknown, and so we progress from illusion to illusion. The winds of folly and desolation howl about us; the sorrows of happiness are the worst to bear, and the wise soon learn that there is nothing to dream of but the end of desire . . .
>
> The manifestation of modern pessimism in John Norton has been described, and how its influence was checked [in his case] by constitutional mysticity has also been shown. Schopenhauer, when he overstepped the line ruled by the Church, was instantly rejected. From him John Norton's faith suffered nothing . . . (132ff).

Although John Norton is led by his Martyn-like 'constitutional mysticity' into finding in the church 'one shelter from the misery and meanness of life', what matters is the fact that his pessimism specifically and demonstrably derives from Schopenhauer. Moore no doubt names Schopenhauer in that odd way because his words in the passage just quoted amount to a paraphrase of many passages in the Fourth Book of *The World as Will and Idea*, which in turn confirms that the 'unbearable burden' does in fact come from there:

> We saw that the inner being of unconscious nature is a constant striving without end and without rest. And this appears to us much more distinctly when we consider the nature of . . . man. Willing and striving is its whole being . . . But the basis of all willing is need, deficiency, and thus pain. Consequently, the nature of . . . man is subject to pain originally and through its very being. If, on the other hand, it lacks objects of desire . . . a terrible void and ennui comes over it, i.e. its being and existence itself becomes an unbearable burden to it. Thus its life swings like a pendulum backwards and forwards between pain and ennui . . . Thus between desiring and attaining all human life flows on throughout. The wish is, in its nature, pain; the attainment soon begets satiety: the end was only apparent; possession takes away the charm; the wish, the need, presents itself under a new form; when it does not, then follows desolateness, emptiness, ennui, against which the conflict is just as painful as against want. (*WWI*, I, 402, 404f).

There is another likely source in Schopenhauer for part of Moore's description of John Norton's pessimism. The words 'When we attain the object of our desire, we must perforce neglect it in favour of something still unknown, and so we progress from illusion to illusion' strongly suggest that Moore also read that addendum to the Fourth Book entitled 'On the Vanity and Suffering of Life', where he will have found the words 'Life presents itself as a continual deception in small things as in great. If it has promised, it does not keep its word, unless to show how little worth desiring were the things desired: thus we are deluded now by hope, now by what was hoped for . . . continual illusion and disillusion' (*WWI*, III, 382f). Although there are a number of similar passages in Schopenhauer's work, the parallel is so close that it amounts to virtual certainty that Moore read 'On the Vanity and Suffering of Life.'

It may be that John Norton's faith had 'suffered nothing' from Schopenhauer, but this does not alter the fact that Moore goes on to describe Norton's view of life in terms which are, in a general way, very close to Schopenhauer: 'his belief in the misery and degradation of earthly life, and the natural bestiality of man, was incurable . . . when . . . the veil fell, and he understood, he was filled with loathing of life' (135). He is saved from the 'plain paganism' of a Schopenhauer by his mysticity, which is reminiscent of Huysmans' conflation of Schopenhauer and Catholicism; and when he undergoes a religious crisis, it is Schopenhauer's view of existence that it brought home to him, for 'the worthlessness and the abjectness of earthly life struck him with awful and all-convincing power' (137). He is cured of his pessimism by falling in love with Kitty Hare; when he loses her, what remains is a vision of Nirvana:

> Yesterday I had all things . . . Today I have nothing; all my hopes are shattered, all my illusions have fallen. So it is always with him who places his trust in life.
>
> Ah, life, life, what hast thou for giving save cruel deceptions and miserable wrongs? Ah, why did I leave my life of contemplation and prayer to enter into that of desire . . . Ah, I knew, well I knew there was no happiness save in calm and contemplation (273).

The rhetorical theatricality here is all Moore's. How Schopenhauer, who wrote in 'The Way of Salvation' that 'There is only one inborn error, and that is, that we exist in order to be happy' (*WWI*, III, 460) would have deplored that word 'happiness'; but, that said, there can be little doubt that what Moore is verbalising here is the 'calm will-less knowledge that Schopenhauer holds up to us as the highest ideal to be attained' (*A Drama in Muslin*, 166). For John Norton (whose story recurs in *Celibates*, 1895), as for Schopenhauer, celibacy is the 'first and most important step in the denial of the will to live' (*WWI*, III, 437).

While it is important to recognise the echoes of Schopenhauer in *A Mere Accident* for what they are, John Norton's brand of asceticism has little in common with Schopenhauer; the Catholicism and the Sussex background obtrude too much for that. Ultimately such charm and depth as the book has, have more to do with Moore's sensitive and skilful evocation of the Latin Middle Ages than to anything to do with Schopenhauer. Like the *Confessions*, in other words, it owes much more to Pater than to Schopenhauer. That Moore was, however, by no means dissatisfied with his Schopenhauer-inspired passages is suggested by the fact that every one of them was taken over into the reworked version of the story which appeared in *Celibates* in 1895 (364ff, 411f,, 444). The dialogue on Latin writers, on the other hand, was replaced by a passage reflecting Moore's new-found enthusiasm for Wagner, with which Schopenhauer was doubtless deemed to be compatible.

It is time now to return to the *Confessions of a Young Man*, the first edition of which appeared in 1888, some months after *Spring Days*, and the second edition shortly afterwards, in order to see whether there is any truth in Moore's statement that the philosophy of the book is that of Schopenhauer. The opening lines of this fictionalized autobiography go some way towards explaining Moore's statement about the philosophy of the book:

> My soul, so far as I understand it, has very kindly taken colour and form from the many various modes of life that self-will and an impetuous temperament have forced me to indulge in. Therefore I may say that I am free from original qualities . . . What I have . . . chance bestowed . . . upon me. (1)

Although the typically Moorish expression, and the generality of what is expressed, make it difficult to be sure, it may well be that what Moore has in mind here is the statement in that section of Schopenhauer's work which he knew best ('The Assertion and Denial of the Will to Live'), that 'everything may be regarded as irrevocably determined by fate' (*WWI*, I, 389). Moore had, after all, as Walter Pater first noted, a deeply felt preference for 'the personal and uncontrollable,' 'the opinion and sensation one cannot help',[46] and Hone was surely right to see this as a pointer to the attraction which Schopenhauer's philosophy had for Moore at this time. Moore himself wrote in the *Confessions* 'Never could I interest myself in a book if it were not the exact diet my mind required at the time' (35), and the diet he needed in 1888 evidently included Schopenhauer's emphasis on the blindness of the Will, on the role of chance in life, and on the primacy of instinct and the irrational intellect. There must have been those who held the view that George Moore was the very embodiment of the irrational intellect; does he not himself speak of the 'reduction of the intellect to the blind unconsciousness of the lower organs' in *Confessions* (3rd Edn., 46)? No doubt the idea that he, George Moore, *was* the world, also appealed to him. Although there is no reason to suppose that there is much detailed knowledge of Schopenhauer's arguments lying behind them, Moore's opening words in *Confessions of a Young Man* probably convinced *him* that his new book was in fact based on Schopenhauer's philosophy. And so in a general sense it was, for Schopenhauer saw the individual as having little control over his own destiny; in 'The Objectification of the Will', he wrote that 'the individual . . . is . . . determined . . . everyone . . . is . . . subjected to necessity . . . he must carry out the very character which he himself condemns' (*WWI*, I, 147). Moore's opening sentence may well be a reaction to this. His use of the word 'soul', however, is proof that he did not read very much of Schopenhauer, who had strong views concerning the use of this word (ibid., III, 105). Further proof of his non-reading of Schopenhauer comes later in the *Confessions* when he writes 'were Hell a reality' (80); Schopenhauer knew that it was a reality: 'The world is a *hell* and human beings are the tortured souls on the one hand, and the devils on the other' (*P&P*: 'Additional Remarks on the Doctrine of the Suffering of the World'). Although Moore seems not to have known this passage, there is some slight evidence that he may have known the *Parerga und Paralipomena* from the French translation of 1880, which would also make it possible that he knew Schopenhauer's comment (in the 'Psychological Remarks') that 'Everything original . . . in man . . . operates unconsciously'. This is at all events the point he is making at the beginning of *Confessions*.

The other echoes of Schopenhauer in *Confessions* are, fortunately, far more specific. The first comes in Chapter III, when Moore writes 'all this I suffered until the burden of unachieved desire grew intolerable' (2nd Edn., 63), which takes us back to the 'unbearable burden' of *A Mere Accident* and its source in the Fourth Book of *The World as Will and Idea*. Schopenhauer, it is true, writes of life becoming an unbearable burden to man when he lacks objects of desire, rather than when his desires remain unfulfilled, but the source of Moore's phrase remains.

Schopenhauer is named in Chapter 9, in a passage which is interesting because it shows Schopenhauer being enlisted in aid of Moore-the-symbolist:

> Not the thing itself, but the idea of the thing evokes the idea [The 3rd edition has 'evoke: the idea']. Schopenhauer was right; we do not want the thing, but the idea of the thing. The thing itself is worthless . . . You want the idea drawn out of obscuring matter, this can best be done by the symbol. (2nd Edn., 231).

Susan Dick has said of this passage that 'Moore invokes Schopenhauer here in a way which also suggests Wagner's theories of art. Wagner, himself deeply affected by Schopenhauer's writings, said: "In daily life the mere sight of an object leaves us cold and unconcerned, and only when we become aware of that object's bearings on our will does it call forth an emotion".'[47] In the present context, however, this does not seem to be the point, for what is in question is the relation of the idea to the Will in Schopenhauer's sense, not to the will in Wagner's everyday sense. What Moore had in mind was almost certainly Schopenhauer's view of music. Whether the misprint in the 1888 version ('evokes the idea'), which reduces the first sentence to gobbledegook, is a reflection of Moore's somewhat tenuous grasp on Schopenhauer's idea, must remain matter for speculation. What is certain is that the sentence, duly corrected in the 1889 edition, paraphrases Schopenhauer's words 'what [the poet] . . . wishes by his work to make us know, is the (Platonic) Idea' ('On the Aesthetics of Poetry,' *WWI*, III, 203f.), although the point is such a general one that the addition of Schopenhauer's name is needed to signal Moore's source. More original is the use to which he puts the idea, which recalls the point made by Hone:

> At this time [1888] Schopenhauer had great vogue in France . . . and Rémy de Gourmont has described the intoxication with which the Symbolists received the revelation that the world was bad and yet existed only relatively to themselves.[48]

It is, I think, safe to assume that Moore's linking of Schopenhauer and Symbolism derives from Paris via Dujardin. Dujardin championed Symbolism in general and Mallarmé (whom Moore also knew) in particular.

The other echo of Schopenhauer in the 1888 edition is very different, although it occurs in the same chapter. Moore has been telling a story about man's 'liking for dirty stories'; having finished his story he tags on a conclusion which is out of all proportion to the triviality of what has gone before, when he writes:

> An awful and terrifying proof of the futility of human effort, that there is neither bad work nor good work to do, nothing but to avoid the coming of the Nirvana. (2nd Edn., 239)

This really amounts to little more than the flaunting of ideas which Moore saw as typical of the 1880s, for while the remark has two close parallels in *The World as Will and Idea*, particularly in the section 'On the Vanity and Suffering of Life' (III, e.g. 383), it sounds rather posey and is certainly uncalled-for in its context. The previous point, on the other hand, is precisely what would prompt Moore to claim that the philosophy of the second edition of the *Confessions* was that of Schopenhauer, although the book in fact owes more to Shelley, Pater and Gautier than to Schopenhauer. It is they who remain the major influences in successive editions of the book, although it suits Moore to claim the patronage, first of Schopenhauer, and then of Nietzsche, as these writers came into fashion. Much of Moore's life's work consists in the rewriting of his own life, and he does not spurn the wisdom of hindsight.

If there was therefore some degree of truth in Moore's claim, what about his further claim that he accentuated this philosophy in revising the *Confessions* for the third (1889) edition? This, let it be said straightaway, is unambiguously true, but also highly misleading. We have seen that the second edition contained three echoes of Schopenhauer; the third contains seven. Only in George Moore's mind could the philosophy of either edition be said to be that of Schopenhauer. It is, however, easy to see what has happened: between the second and third editions of the *Confessions* Moore has written a book which *is* based on the philosophy of Schopenhauer: the novel *Mike Fletcher.* Since his head is full of his latest 'fad', he likes to think that *Confessions* is too, though it is not. Nor do the additional allusions to Schopenhauer amount to a matter of the 'utmost importance'. On the contrary, they are trivial.

The first of the relevant additions, 'Terrible and imperative is the voice of the will to live' (3rd Edn., 12), does certainly sound like George Moore tuning his Schopenhauerian voice. At the beginning of the 'decadent' Nineties, let us remember, a portion of Schopenhauerian gloom was still *de rigueur*: in his essay 'The Cultured Faun', published in the *Anti-Jacobin* in 1891, Lionel Johnson wrote: 'To play the part properly a flavour of cynicism is recommended: a scientific profession of materialist dogmas, coupled — for you should forswear consistency — with gloomy chatter about "The Will to Live".'

Longest of the new passages, and more interesting, is a Schopenhauer-inspired discussion of those favourite themes of Moore's early work, celibacy and suicide:

> Besides, marriage is antagonistic to my ideal. You say that no ideal illumines the pessimist's life, that he cannot answer, if you ask him, why he exists, and that Schopenhauer's arguments against suicide are not even plausible casuistry. True, on this point his reasoning is feeble and ineffective. But we may easily confute our sensual opponents. We must say that we do not commit suicide, although we admit it is a certain anodyne to the poison of life, — an absolute erasure of the wrong inflicted on us by our parents, — because we hope by noble example and precept to induce others to refrain from love. We are the saviours of souls. Other crimes are finite; love alone is infinite. (3rd Edn., 342).

No doubt part of this highly subjective passage is vaguely based on Schopenhauer's 'The Metaphysics of the Love of the Sexes' (in *WWI*, III) and on his view of the need to deny the will to live. The 'feeble and ineffective' reasoning with which Moore chides Schopenhauer, on the other hand, involves an allusion to the passage in the Fourth Book of *The World as Will and Idea* (I, 514f) where Schopenhauer argues that suicide, far from involving denial of the will, in fact involves strong assertion of the will. This is the only part of Schopenhauer's argument to which Moore's remarks could apply, so that once again he is alluding to the same section of Schopenhauer's work as on previous occasions. Since he makes much the same point again in *Mike Fletcher*, he must have been under the mistaken impression that he had caught the sage of Frankfurt nodding.

A couple of pages later Moore makes his persona's Conscience ask: 'you go in for [Hartmann's] "The Philosophy of the Unconscious"?'

The answer is characteristic:

> No, no, 'tis but a silly vulgarisation. But Schopenhauer, oh, my Schopenhauer! Say, shall I go about preaching hatred of women? Were I to call them a short-legged race that was admitted into society only a hundred and fifty years ago? (3rd Edn., 344).

We have already seen that Moore knew Hartmann's *Philosophy of the Unconscious*, which he himself evidently regarded as a 'silly vulgarisation' of Schopenhauer's more aesthetic philosophy. What is so interesting here is the fact that Moore's criticism of Schopenhauer's remarks on suicide presumably derives from Hartmann, who makes the same point (*Philosophy of the Unconscious*, repr. 1931, III, 100f).

Turning to Schopenhauer, it is interesting to discover that Moore knew of Schopenhauer's words 'Only the male intellect, clouded by the sexual impulse, could call the undersized, narrow-shouldered, broad-hipped and short-legged sex the fair sex' (*P&P*: 'On Women'). He most likely heard of this, the best-known passage of Schopenhauer's work, in the Paris of the early 1880s, from Dujardin; or he may have read it in Cantacuzène's selection from *Parerga und Paralipomena* (there was no English translation of *Parerga und Paralipomena* in existence at that time) or in Jean Bourdeau's famous anthology. Otherwise he could have read the passage in the 'Notes sur Schopenhauer' by Jean Moréas in *La Revue Indépendante* (1886),[49] or he could have heard of it from one or other of the *Médanistes*. Be this as it may, if Schopenhauer's words arguably deserved no better than they got, it is typical of Moore first to apostrophize Schopenhauer, and then, in the very next breath, to trivialize him.

In the last of the four additional passages which were said to accentuate the Schopenhauerian philosophy of this third edition we read:

> If you had read Schopenhauer [Moore tells himself, with perhaps greater irony than he realised] you would know that the flesh is not ephemeral, but the eternal objectification of the will to live. Siva is represented, not only with the necklace of skulls, but with the lingam. (3rd Edn., 346f).

Moore is here paraphrasing from 'The Assertion and Denial of the Will' (*WWI*, I, 355f), where Schopenhauer wrote:

> Birth and death belong merely to the phenomenon of will, thus to life; and it is essential to this to exhibit itself in individuals which come into being and pass away, as fleeting phenomena appearing in the form of time — phenomena of that which in itself knows no time, but must exhibit itself precisely in the way we have said, in order to objectify its peculiar nature. Birth and death belong in like manner to life . . . The wisest of all mythologies, the Indian, expresses this by giving to . . . Siva as an attribute not only the necklace of skulls, but also the lingam . . .

What Moore wrote in the Preface to the third edition of *Confessions* — 'I owe much of my mind to Schopenhauer; but I will not say here that if these confessions induce anyone to turn to "The World as Will and Idea", they will have effected their purpose. My book was written to be read, not to help another book to be read' — is interesting as tending to confirm that it was mainly from *The World as Will and Idea*, as translated by Haldane and Kemp, whose title he quotes, that he derived his first-hand knowledge of Schopenhauer. Otherwise his claim needs to be treated with caution. Objectively speaking it is exaggerated to the point of no longer being true; the revision of *Confessions* for the third edition was brilliantly done, but anyone can see that what it accentuates is not so much the philosophy of Schopenhauer as the world of the *Nouvelle Athènes*. It is as well, I think, to remember that Moore, in the *Confessions*, wrote of himself as being as 'covered with "fads" as a distinguished foreigner with stars. Naturalism I wore round my neck, Romanticism was pinned over the heart, Symbolism I carried like a toy revolver in my waistcoat pocket, to be used on an emergency' (2nd Edn., 246; 3rd Edn., 259). This is both candid and relevant, for there is so little of Schopenhauer even in the third edition of *Confessions*, that the conclusion is inescapable that 'Schopenhauer' is not very much more than a word, Moore's current fashionable 'fad'. Had he gone on to write 'Schopenhauer I wore on my sleeve', *that* would have been true. When he writes 'I owe much of my mind to Schopenhauer', he no doubt thinks that this is true, but it is not; whereas Hardy plays down his indebtedness to Schopenhauer, Moore exaggerates his. As so often, Moore is saying what he thinks will sound well; this is what I meant when I said that for him truth was an aesthetic category. His claim reminds me of Schopenhauer's discussion of the difference between conceivability and truth and his definition of the Münchhausenism (*anglice*: tall story), in which

> the fact is always so conceived that when it is thought merely in the abstract, and therefore comparatively *a priori*, it appears possible and plausible; but afterwards, when we come down to the perception of the particular case, *a posteriori* the impossibility of the thing . . . is bought into prominence ('On the Theory of the Ludicrous', *WWI*, II, 278).

At this point let us remember that Moore, for all his 'flaunting' of ideas, and for all his 'fads', was in no sense a philosopher. It is true that John Eglinton, in his 'Recollection of George Moore', recorded his view that Moore was 'almost a philosopher, who found a contemplative satisfaction in looking at life in the spirit of a landscape-painter', but that is another matter. The ideas that can be extrapolated or inferred from his stories do not and cannot be expected to form a philosophical system. They are merely ideas, and not only was Moore's attitude towards ideas ambivalent and frequently ironical, but ideas which are used as building bricks in a novel are necessarily affected by the fictionalization and ironization to which they are subjected. Moore may have gone around covered with 'fads', but he did not wear his heart on his sleeve. Extrapolating a writer's own views from beneath the ironies and fictions of his work is always difficult, if not downright foolhardy. In the case of *Confessions*, for instance, the spate of words suggests that one is faced with straightforward reminiscence; but appearances are deceptive, the author's intentions more complex. In 1888 Moore is, it is true, looking back with pleasure upon the enthusiasms of his past self in Paris. But this is no mere *recherche du temps perdu*, for he has in many ways outgrown the enthusiasm and centres of interest of those heady days; an undercurrent of irony therefore develops. The backward look is moreover counter-balanced by a prospective look. The image of the glorious anarchy of Parisian artistic life is used as a foil to the image of stuffy, hide-bound London literary life, so that *Confessions* is simultaneously an essay in autobiography and self-examination, *and* a fire-ship launched against the Victorian Establishment.[50] As fire-ship the book flies the flag of convenience: in the original Preface the jolly Roger (a rallying signal to like-minded innovators and a challenge to the mercantile fleet of the literary conservatives), in 1889 a Schopenhauerian black flag, in 1904 (because of the general evolution of the age) a Nietzschean one. To a not inconsiderable extent these flags of convenience are also a smoke screen protecting from view the real George Moore, that agnostic with a penchant for mysticity of which he was half-ashamed.

Spring Days appeared in 1888, some months after *Confessions of a Young Man*. Moore described it as 'the tale of a city merchant who is worried about his daughters — a sort of comic King Lear.' The only character in the novel of any interest to us is Frank Escott, heir to an Irish peerage but otherwise a very ordinary man: 'Life had no deep truth for him, no underlying mysteries . . . the philosophic temperament was absent in him' (121). This is really the long and the short of it; Frank Escott is not a thinking man, and *Spring Days* is by no means a philosophical novel. Practically the only trace of philosophy comes in Chapter XIII, when Moore puts into Escott's head uncharacteristic thoughts that are obviously his own and merely show Moore somewhat self- consciously indulging in a piece of fine writing. Frank Escott has just had his engagement broken off by Maggie Brookes, and the passage in question, beginning 'Over the shingle bank the sea faded, a thin illusion, dim and promiseful of peace' and ending 'it is I who am the world' (315f.) represents his unwonted philosophizing at this critical juncture. It is an extraordinary piece of romantic philosophizing to find in a determinedly realistic novel. In a general way the passage belongs together with the Schopenhauer-inspired passages in *A Mere Accident* and *Mike Fletcher*, and indeed with similar passages echoing Nietzsche and Wagner in *Evelyn Innes*. It stands out in the context above all because it consists of thoughts which

Frank Escott would have been quite incapable of thinking. And these thoughts, which are therefore very much Moore's own, contain just one echo of Schopenhauer: that last phrase, 'it is I who am the world.' Of the 'allusions to the philosophy of Schopenhauer' which the book has been said to contain,[51] there is no other sign.

Mike Fletcher was published in 1889, the same year that saw the publication of the novel in which Schopenhauer's impact on George Gissing reached its climax: *The Nether World*. It has been plausibly suggested that Moore may have reworked material from his abandoned novel *Aristocracy of Vice* (*c.* 1880/81) into *Mike Fletcher*, although there is no evidence that this was the case. What concerns us here is not so much the plot of the novel, which is virtually non- existent — a fact which loomed large in the hostile reception it received — as the thoughts of two contrasting characters: Mike Fletcher, editor of *The Pilgrim* (reminiscent of Augustus Moore's *The Hawk*), 'dirty voluptuary' and 'epitome of Western grossness and lust of life', and John Norton, a priggish young Catholic ascete with a penchant for Schopenhauer, Buddhism and the Middle Ages. It is accordingly not an 'aesthetic novel', but a novel of ideas, albeit in the somewhat limited sense that has been so well defined by Farrow as 'the exfoliation of a few simple ideas developed into patterns by characters who embody them under various guises'.[52] In this particular case it is a matter of opposite reactions to Schopenhauer on the part of the voluptuary and the ascete, or, better, a matter of the assertion (Mike Fletcher) and denial (John Norton) of the will to live.

The first reference to Schopenhauer comes in an early discussion between two subsidiary characters, Harding and Escott, 'as to whether Goëthe [sic] had stolen from Schopenhauer, or Schopenhauer from Goëthe, the comparison of man's life with the sun "which seems to set to our earthly eyes, but which in reality never sets, but shines on unceasingly"' (4). What matters here is not the fact that Moore cannot spell Goethe's name, but the fact that the discussion is taken straight from a footnote in the Fourth Book of *The World as Will and Idea*:

> In Eckermann's 'Conversations of Goethe' . . . Goethe says: 'Our spirit is a being of a nature quite indestructible, and its activity continues from eternity to eternity. It is like the sun, which seems to set only to our earthly eyes, but which, in reality, never sets, but shines on unceasingly.' Goethe has taken the simile from me; not I from him (*WWI*, I, 362).

The quotation, which at first glance looks like the sort of gobbet that Hardy used to record in his notebooks and use as padding in his novels, is in fact something far more important: proof positive of Moore's reading of 'The Assertion and Denial of the Will to Live'.

Shortly after this, Harding, 'that cynical atheist', as Moore dubs him, speaks with Schopenhauer when he says that 'the world is but our idea' (5), an idea which Schopenhauer develops later in 'The Assertion and Denial of the Will' (see *WWI*, I, 428). The womanizer Fletcher rejoins, characteristically: 'I suppose it was Schopenhauer's dislike of women that first attracted you. He used to call women the short-legged race, that were only admitted into society a hundred and fifty years ago.' — 'Did he say that?' (6). Harding's ignorance shows that whatever attracted *him* to Schopenhauer, it was not that. The exchange is relatively unimportant; it simply shows Moore re-using a scurrilous remark from *Parerga und Paralipomena* that he had recently used in *Confessions of a Young Man*.

The most interesting thing in the first chapter of *Mike Fletcher*, and the most amusing episode in the whole of the story of Moore and Schopenhauer, is John Norton's confession. Norton goes to confession to confess that he is about to publish 'The Last Struggle', 'a philosophic poem based on Schopenhauer':

> 'I did not catch the name.' [says the priest]
>
> 'Schopenhauer; if you are acquainted with his works, father, you will appreciate my anxieties, and will see just where my difficulty lies.'
>
> 'I cannot say that I can call to mind at this moment any exact idea of his philosophy; does it include a denial of the existence of God?'
>
> 'His teaching, I admit, is atheistic in its tendency, but I do not follow him to his conclusions. A part of his theory — that of the resignation of desire of life — seems to me not only reconcilable with the traditions of the Church, but may really be said to have been original and vital in early Christianity . . . Jesus Christ our Lord is the perfect symbol of the denial of the will to live.' . . .
>
> 'I was anxious, father [John goes on], to give you in a few words some account of the philosophy which has been engaging my attention, so that you might better understand my difficulties. Although Schopenhauer may be wrong in his theory regarding the will, the conclusions he draws from it, namely, that we may only find lasting peace in resignation, seems to me well within the dogma of our holy Church.'
>
> 'It surprises me that he should hold such opinions, for if he does not acknowledge a future state, the present must be everything, and the gratification of the senses the only . . .'
>
> 'I assure you, father, no one can be more opposed to materialism than Schopenhauer. He holds the world we live in to be a mere delusion — the veil of Maya.'
>
> 'I am afraid, my son, I cannot speak with any degree of certainty about either of those authors, but I think it my duty to warn you against inclining too willing an ear to the specious sophistries of German philosophers . . . I have forgotten the name.'
>
> 'Schopenhauer.'
>
> 'Now I will give you absolution.' (9f.)

Moore's satire here can best be left to speak for itself; all I would add is that it is not until one gets to P.G. Wodehouse[53] that a humorous note re-enters the story of Schopenhauer's impact on English literature.

John Norton, with 'his pessimism, his Catholicism, his yearning for ritual, his . . . hatred of women' (43) is an interesting but distant figure. Though based on Moore's cousin Edward Martyn, he is also, in some ways, reminiscent of Schopenhauer himself. I am thinking of his misogynism, his ascetism, his remarks about the connexions between Christianity and Buddhism, and indeed the Buddha in his room. Following his confession

John Norton burnt his 'pessimistic poem' for the entirely 'Schopenhauerian' reason that 'I can only attain salvation by the elimination of all responsibilities' (10) — a point of view which is analysed at some length at the end of 'The Assertion and Denial of the Will'. On renouncing Schopenhauer he becomes more of a Schopenhauerian than ever. He presently tells Mike Fletcher that:

> Now the very name of Schopenhauer revolts me. I accept nothing of his ideas. From that ridiculous pessimism I have drifted very far indeed. Pessimism is impossible. To live we must have an ideal, and pessimism offers none . . . Schopenhauer's arguments against suicide are not valid, that you admit, therefore it is impossible for the pessimist to justify his continued existence (128).

After this John Norton fades out of the novel, although not before we have been given to understand that he has 'embrace[d] the cloister' (261), thereby becoming the embodiment of Schopenhauer's ideal, the denial of the will.

The field is therefore left to Mike Fletcher, who, it transpires, is writing 'a poem on Schopenhauer's philosophy' (45). When considering Fletcher it needs to be remembered that he is really not so much a follower of Schopenhauer, as an embodiment of the assertion of the will to live. Read thus, his otherwise senseless words and actions make sense. For it is, as John Norton says, hard to associate pessimism with the Mike Fletcher of the beginning of the novel:

> Only because you take the ordinary view of the tendency of pessimistic teaching [said Mike]. If you want a young and laughing world, preach Schopenhauer at every street corner . . . The pessimist believes that forgetfulness and nothingness is the whole of man. He says 'I defy the wisest of you to tell me why I am here, and being here, what good is gained by my assisting to bring others here.' The pessimist is therefore the gay Johnny (45f.)

One is reminded of the remark attributed to a friend of Eduard von Hartmann and related by Francis Bowen in his *Modern Philosophy from Descartes to Schopenhauer and Hartmann*, which Moore could have read since it came out in 1877: 'If you wish to see bright and contented faces, you must go among the Pessimists'.[54] John Norton's shriek of laughter at this point in the proceedings is understandable, especially when Mike goes on to describe his Schopenhauerian poem in the following terms:

> Man has at last recognised that life is in equal parts misery and abomination, and has resolved that it shall cease. The tide of passion has again risen . . . but knowledge — calm, will-less knowledge — has gradually invaded all hearts . . . it is man's natural and inveterate stupidity (Schopenhauer calls it Will) that forces man to live and continue his species. (46, 52).

A number of things become clear as Mike Fletcher goes on, notably that he is, alas, a *persona* of the abominable Moore, whose words he repeats (that 'calm, will-less knowledge' first appeared in *A Drama in Muslin*), and that he has very little understanding of Schopenhauer. Mike Fletcher's main concern becomes that typical obsession of the 1880s, suicide, although before his final self-assertion, he first causes the suicide of Lady Helen Seymour by teaching her to read Schopenhauer. He tells her that 'Schopenhauer is wrong' about suicide (87), repeating the point made in *Confessions*. A little later he spells out his ideas. First he agrees with Schopenhauer:

> There are two forces in human nature — instinct and reason. The first is the very principle of life, and exists in all we see — give it a philosophic name, and call it the 'will to live'. All, therefore, proceed from instinct or from reason. Suicide is clearly not an instinctive act, it is therefore a reasonable act; and being of all acts the least instinctive, it is of necessity the most reasonable; reason and instinct are antagonistic; and the extreme point of their antagonism must clearly be suicide. One is the assertion of life, the other is the denial of life' (274).

Then he disagrees with him: 'suicide . . . is a protest against all life' (ibid). Schopenhauer himself had argued that 'The suicide . . . by no means surrenders the will to live' (*WWI*, I, 514ff). Writing on Schopenhauer's philosophy in Dujardin's *Revue Indépendante* in March 1885, Félix Féneon had stressed this point: 'Quiconque se tue veut la vie; il ne se plaint que des conditions dans lesquelles elle s'offre à lui.' It has even been argued that 'The entire novel is a careful dramatization of Schopenhauer's theory of suicide',[55] although it would be more to the point, I think, to say that the novel is a dramatization of Schopenhauer's ideas on the assertion and denial of the will to live.

Mike Fletcher continues to echo George Moore when he addresses to John Norton views which once again repeat, pretty well word for word, remarks attributed to Moore's *persona* in the *Confessions*:

> Pessimism . . . offers the highest [ideal] — not to create life is the only good; the creation of life is the only evil; all else which man in his bestial stupidity calls good and evil is ephemeral and illusionary . . . the diffusion of the principle of sufficient reason can alone end this world, and we are justified in living in order that by example and precept we may dissuade others from the creation of life. The incomparable stupidity of life teaches us to love our parents — divine philosophy teaches us to forgive them. (*Mike Fletcher*, 128).

Even allowing for the fact that he is satirizing Fletcher by making him vulgarize Schopenhauer in this way, it does seem that Moore was right to blame his subject in this novel, and that the novel got out of hand because he gave too much space to ideas which he was, for part of the time at least, only prepared to vulgarize. He is out of his element and maybe out of his depth, although *The Brook Kerith* shows that eventually, with the help of Dujardin, he came to terms with the most important of the ideas in question.

As Mike's thoughts float 'in the boundless atmosphere of Schopenhauer's poem, of the denial of the will to live' (234), Schopenhauer drifts in and out of focus:

> We cannot desire what we possess, and so we progress from illusion to illusion. But when we cease to distinguish between ourself and others, when our thoughts are no longer set on the consideration of our own embarrassed condition, when we see into the heart of things, which is one, then disappointment and suffering cease to have any meaning, and we attain that true serenity and peace which we sometimes see reflected in a seraph's face by Raphael. (234)

The first sentence here, which we first encountered in a slightly different form in *A Mere Accident*, derives, as we have already seen, from one of the addenda to the Fourth Book of *The World as Will and Idea*, 'On the Vanity and Suffering of Life'. Its re-use here suggests that Moore was impressed by what he read in Schopenhauer. The rest of the passage is taken from Moore's usual source, 'The Assertion and Denial of the Will to Live', at the end of which Schopenhauer wrote:

> But if we turn our glance from our own needy and embarrassed condition to those who have overcome the world, in whom the will, having attained to perfect self-knowledge, found itself again in all, and then freely denied itself, and who then merely wait to see the last trace of it vanish with the body which it animates; then instead of the restless striving and effort, instead of the constant transition from wish to fruition, and from joy to sorrow, instead of the never-satisfied and never-dying hope which constitutes the life of the man who wills, we shall see that peace which is above all reason, that perfect calm of the spirit, that deep rest, that inviolable confidence and serenity, the mere reflection of which in the countenance, as Raphael and Correggio have represented it, is an entire and certain gospel; only knowledge remains, the will has vanished. (*WWI*, I, 531).

These remarks define the ideal by which John Norton lives, an ideal which Mike Fletcher can define in another man's words but can never hope to understand. They are followed, in terms of echoes of Schopenhauer, by a remark ('Since I became a student of Schopenhauer I have given up waltzing. Now I never indulge in anything but a square': *Mike Fletcher*, 257) which is plain silly.

And so we come to the end of this moral degenerate who had

> drifted too far into the salt sea of unfaith and cynicism, ever to gain again the fair if illusive shores of aspiration — maybe illusive, but no more illusive than the cruel sea that swung him like a wreck in its current . . . Nor could he make surrender of his passion of life, saying — 'I see into the heart of things, I know the truth, and in the calm possession of knowledge am able to divest myself of my wretched individuality, and so free myself of all evils, seeking in absorption, rather than by violent ends to rid myself of consciousness.' (279).

Fletcher's words are not a quotation from Schopenhauer, but rather a paraphrase of Schopenhauer's exposition of the denial of the will (*WWI*, III, 420–467); more particularly they are a description of Schopenhauer's 'self-renunciation', which has nothing to do with suicide. This brings us to the point which Moore immediately proceeds to make: 'But this, the religion of the truly wise, born in the sublime East, could find no roothold in Mike Fletcher — that type and epitome of Western grossness and lust of life' (*Mike Fletcher*, 279). In the present context this is more important than the following reference to 'the demoralizing influence of the introduction of Eastern pessimism into a distinctly Western nature' (280), although it must not be forgotten that the discovery of Schopenhauer and Buddhism affected the suicide statistics in the 1880s. Unlike John Norton, who belongs among the 'truly wise' who are able to deny the will, Mike Fletcher could only assert his wretched will in the one way that remained to him. That he does so, proves that Schopenhauer had *not* got it wrong. Fletcher's final thought echoes Schopenhauer in pointing to the cause of mankind's misery (desire), but the metaphor of which it forms part ('Like a gray beast [day] comes on soft velvet paws to devour . . . light and desire are the claws that the . . . beast unsheathes': 287) seems to point forward to Yeats' 'The Second Coming' and therefore to a more general apocalypse.

George Moore, a particularly unreliable judge of his own work, tended to think that each successive book was the best yet; in the case of *Mike Fletcher* the hostile reviews soon made him change his mind, and he came to speak of it as 'that awful book', 'a detestable book'.[56] Indeed, he bitterly regretted publishing it. In letters to Mme Lanza he wrote:

> I realize now that *Mike Fletcher* is not good. I wish I had known how bad it was and I wouldn't have published it . . . My next novel will be more human. I shall bathe myself in the simplest and most naive emotions, the daily bread of humanity.[57]

Mike Fletcher was the only one of his novels which he chose not to revise and of which he did not even speak, although he did allow it to be reissued in 1899. Moore himself put the blame on the subject, which is all very well, but what the reader cannot fail to notice is that Mike Fletcher himself is an extremely uninteresting, and indeed boring figure. The references to Schopenhauer, almost all of them duly labelled with the philosopher's name, do, it is true, amount to something more than the kind of seasoning which such references in the previous novels had been. But they remain problematical, as do Schopenhauer's ideas, which, despite the often brilliantly witty and therefore amusing expression, cannot be said to make for cheerful reading. If they are used as seasoning in a novel, it is not so bad; when, as in *Mike Fletcher*, they form the whole structural basis of the novel, it is very bad indeed. When fictionalized and thereby vulgarized, they tend to be morbid, maudlin, melodramatic. We have seen that George

Moore was content, for a time, to 'flaunt' his ideas, but even in *Mike Fletcher* he was not 'influenced' by Schopenhauer so much as carried away by him. That Schopenhauer's ideas can be used successfully, though not to cheerful effect, was shown by George Gissing; but then he, unlike George Moore, was a real Schopenhauer-enthusiast. Adopting a remark of his to John Eglinton,[58] one might venture the opinion that in *Mike Fletcher* Moore 'lost his talent in philosophic . . . hallucinations.' In the present context the novel is important for two related reasons: because it is the one novel by Moore which actually uses Schopenhauer's ideas as architectonic material, being 'insistently interlaced with the spirit and teachings of the German sage',[59] and because it contains the seed of a better, more important and more characteristic work: *The Brook Kerith*.

Notwithstanding *The Brook Kerith*, however, it is true to say that with *Mike Fletcher* Moore's preoccupation with Schopenhauer shot its bolt, although in the essay on Balzac written in 1889, first published in the *Fortnightly Review* (December 1889) and then used as the first chapter of *Impressions and Opinions* (1891), there are, not surprisingly, some remaining echoes of his cult of Schopenhauer, echoes which were duly excised in the new edition of *Impressions and Opinions* in 1913. The main allusion to Schopenhauer in the essay on Balzac comes when Moore celebrates Balzac's imaginative strength in the words 'The world is but man's thought'. He then goes on to write:

> Never shall I forget the emotions, strangling in their intensity, with which I read those last pages of *Le Lys dans la Vallée* — those pages in which the calm frenzy of renunciation is expressed, — that scene when the priest enters and exhorts, and when we see the heroine falling from her passion and desire until nothing is left but the pure will-less soul of the saint. This death is but the representation of the philosophy of the abnegation of self, which Schopenhauer taught as being the only gate through which lasting happiness may be found.

Is it fanciful to see here the germ of *Evelyn Innes*?

In Moore's next novel, *Vain Fortune* (1892) there are no references to Schopenhauer, and the occasional use of 'Schopenhauerian' phrases has no further significance. The ending of the novel ('she came, offering herself as compensation for the burden of life') echoed a fad which Moore had already outgrown, even if he was not yet ready to signal the fact; John Norton reappears in *Celibates* (1895), but did not make it into *Celibate Lives* (1927).

Whether *Evelyn Innes* (1898) was connected in Moore's mind with the Balzac essay or not, the novel contains a few faint echoes of Schopenhauer. Thus Ulick Dean, who was 'only attracted by essential ideas', thinks of 'The comedy of existence . . . the striving and yearning, and then the inevitable acceptation of the burden of life; in other words, the entrance into the life of resignation' (190). Evelyn's rôles similarly involve echoes of Schopenhauer (via the 'most celebrated of the living Schopenhauerians', Wagner): Isolde is described as the will to live, (151) and her Margaret's 'desire to possess' (162) is described in terms which, reminiscent of the earlier novels as they are, show Schopenhauer appropriated. When Evelyn herself attains the life of resignation, the thoughts with which we leave her are again Schopenhaueresque: 'The world exists not in itself, but in man's thought' (479). These are, however, incidental echoes in what is essentially a Wagnerian novel, as 'rotten with Wagnerism' as Moore himself claimed to be; in the continuation of *Evelyn Innes*, *Sister Teresa* (1901), even the bullfinches are made to whistle Wagnerian motives![60]

So far as the plays of the period are concerned, there are, similarly, a few vague echoes of Schopenhauer in *The Strike at Arlingford* (1893) and *The Bending of the Bough* (1900). In *The Strike at Arlingford* Baron Steinbach, the capitalist, takes what could be called a 'Schopenhauerian' view of life in arguing that 'The misery of man is incurable' (95); but there is nothing in the play that has any specific connexion with Schopenhauer or with Sully, who headed one of his pages on Schopenhauer 'Life's misery irremediable'. In *The Bending of the Bough*, for its part, Moore puts into Kirwan's mouth the words 'Life, always hungry, follows eager to devour us', which are 'Schopenhauerian' enough in a general sense, particularly since Kirwan goes on to say 'Woman is life in its most typical form and family life a wolfish pack' and 'life is what we should flee from'. The remark about Woman is virtually a summary of Schopenhauer's thesis in the 'Metaphysics of Love' (*WWI*, Book IV), with the 'wolfish pack' being a Moorish extrapolation from Schopenhauer's *homo homini lupus* theme. The idea that life is 'what we should flee from' is the theme of another chapter of that same Fourth Book, 'On the Denial of the Will to Live'. Similarly the young Celtophile, Dean Swift, is made to say 'Do we not all follow chimeras . . .? Is it so sure that the material world which he follows is less chimerical than the spiritual truths which I strive to follow . . . At all events we have no proof that spiritual truths are illusory, whereas we know that the world is.' While this is reminiscent of Schopenhauer's view of the world in a general way, there is nothing specifically Schopenhauerian about the play. Neither the ineffectual young 'hero' nor his mentor embodies a Schopenhauerian attitude to life, and the comedy as a whole has absolutely nothing to do with Schopenhauer. These are isolated ideas, *voilà tout*. They mark the end of the superficial stage of Moore's preoccupation with the German philosopher; the real, and lasting, influence of Schopenhauer is seen in *The Brook Kerith* (1916).

In *The Brook Kerith* Moore returned to what, in *Mike Fletcher*, he had called 'the religion of the truly wise, born in the sublime East.' In returning to Eastern quietism he was returning, as we have seen, to a Schopenhauer long since assimilated. Now in warning readers against attaching too much importance to the influence of Schopenhauer on Moore, Hone went on to write that:

> Moore . . . shared and continued to share the Frankfurt philosopher's aversion from Judaism and belief in the superior wisdom of India. Years later the Jesus of the end of *The Brook Kerith* was to be conceived as a sort of Buddhist sage to whom all desire, even the desire of God, is evil[61]

This important general point is borne out by *The Brook Kerith* itself, in the final pages of which we read: 'Paul began to trace a likeness between the doctrines that Jesus had confided to him and . . . the doctrines that were being preached by the monks from India . . . The monks from India will . . . gather from him that he divined much of their philosophy.' The point is of fundamental importance in Schopenhauer's discussion of Christianity; in 'On the Doctrine of the Denial of the Will to Live' he wrote quite specifically that 'I . . . cannot give up the belief that the doctrines of Christianity can . . . be derived from [Brahmanism and Buddhhism]' (*WWI*, III, 445), and he constantly returns to the subject, discussing it at length in 'On Religion'. On the evidence of *The Brook Kerith*, the real influence of Schopenhauer on George Moore has its source there.

The connexion in Moore's mind between Schopenhauer and *The Brook Kerith* was perhaps revealed by the story he once told about *The Apostle*, the stage version of *The Brook Kerith*:

> He once told how he had forced himself to delete from *The Apostle* . . . a moving but irrelevant scene in which Paul bade farewell to Eunice. He reminded himself, he said, of Schopenhauer's wise saying that in great art the merely charming is never found, and he composed an epigram of his own: 'In art we are always sacrificing good things. A plague upon good things! for they profit us nothing in the end.'[62]

Schopenhauer's saying is to be found in his 'On the Inner Nature of Art' (*WWI*, III, 180f.); in *Conversations in Ebury Street*, (Chapter XIX) we read of 'Schopenhauer's wise words: The merely charming is never found in great art'.

Now whether or not this story reveals it, there is certainly a connexion between *The Brook Kerith* and Schopenhauer, and this connexion shows that *The Brook Kerith* has its origin in *Mike Fletcher*, in the various passages in which John Norton argues that what Schopenhauer wrote about the need for resignation of desire 'seems to me not only reconcilable with the traditions of the Church, but may really be said to have been original and vital in early Christianity' (*Mike Fletcher*, 10), and more especially in Norton's conviction that 'Jesus Christ Our Lord is the perfect symbol of the denial of the will to live' (ibid.). To those who know only his diatribes against degenerate, dogmatic Christianity, and more particularly against his *bête noire*, the Church of England, it may come as a surprise to learn that in the chapter entitled 'On the Doctrine of the Denial of the Will to Live' in the Fourth Book of *The World as Will and Idea* Schopenhauer argued very forcefully that 'The inmost kernal and spirit of Christianity is identical with that of Brahmanism and Buddhism' (*WWI*, III, 421); more specifically he stated that 'the ascetic spirit of the denial of one's self. . . is the fundamental characteristic which Christianity has in common with Brahmanism and Buddhism, and which proves their relationship' (*WWI*, III, 447). The basic point is reiterated:

> Christianity in essential respects, taught only what all Asia knew long before . . . It taught the great truth of the assertion and denial of the will to live in the clothing of allegory . . . That great fundamental truth, then, which is contained in Christianity, as in Brahmanism and Buddhism, the need of deliverance from an existence which is given up to suffering and death, and the attainableness of this by the denial of the will (*WWI*, III, 451f)

Earlier, in 'The Assertion and Denial of the Will', Schopenhauer made precisely John Norton's point: that 'Jesus Christ ought always to be conceived . . . as the symbol or personification of the denial of the will to live' (*WWI*, I, 524). At this stage let us remember that Schopenhauer makes a sharp distinction between Christianity proper (or Christian ethics), which he derives from Brahmanism and Buddhism and which he associates with the denial of the will, and, on the other hand, what he calls the Jewish dogmatic element in Christianity. With the former he identifies to the point of regarding himself as a Christian philosopher *par excellence*: 'my ethical teaching agrees with that of Christianity, completely and in its highest tendencies' (*WWI*, III, 474). His exposition of the 'Denial of the Will to Live' ends not with the bare fact of human suffering, but with Meister Eckhard's 'The swiftest animal that bears thee to perfection is suffering' (*WWI*, III, 459).

Schopenhauer argues, moreover, that Sakya Muni and Meister Eckhard teach the same (*WWI*, III, 434). This brings us to the very kernal of *The Brook Kerith*, in which Moore makes his Jesus not only see men as 'the dupes of illusion and desire', but go on to argue that 'God is but desire, and whosoever yields to desire falls into sin. To be without sin we must be without God.' Jesus is so startled at the thoughts that had been put into his mind that he wondered whether 'any man had dared to ask himself if God were not indeed the last uncleanness of the mind' (Chapter XXX). Notwithstanding a few 'Zarathustran' images in *The Brook Kerith* (the cave opening between rocks in Chapter XXXVIII points back to what Moore called 'the sundered rocks about the cave of Zarathoustra'; the eagle in the midday sky in Chapter XL is a recurrent motif in *Zarathustra*), this is not an indistinct echo of Nietzsche's 'death of God', although the violence of the phrase 'the last uncleanness of the mind' may sound Nietzschean enough, particularly when one remembers that Moore, at the time of *The Brook Kerith*, wrote to John Eglinton: 'Are you aware that Jesus was one of the most terrifying fanatics that ever lived in the world, that he out-Nietzsched Nietzsche in the awful things he says in the Gospel of Luke? . . . he shocked me much more than anything in Nietzsche'.[63] On the contrary, this is pure Schopenhauer, the doctrine of the denial of the will to live taken to a logical extreme; even the language is reminiscent of Schopenhauer, who is far more articulate than Nietzsche. Moore's passage belongs together with the passage in 'On the Doctrine of the Denial of the Will to Live' in which Schopenhauer quotes Meister Eckhard's precept for the perfect ascetic: 'that he seek not God outside himself' (*WWI*, III, 432). The idea that 'The pursuit of an incorruptible crown leads to sin as much as the pursuit of a corruptible crown. If we would reach the sinless state we must relinquish pursuit' (*The Brook Kerith*, Chapter XLI) is but a summary of the part of *The World as Will and Idea* that Moore knew best, in other words, the Fourth Book. Schopenhauer wrote there that 'The Christian mystic and the teacher of the Vedanta philosophy agree in this respect also, [that] they both regard all outward works and religious exercises as superfluous for him who has attained to perfection' (*WWI*, I, 503). Moore's indebtedness to Schopenhauer, which is beyond all possible doubt, is, unnecessarily, signalled in the way we might expect: by Jesus's use of that familiar phrase, 'the burden of life' (Chapter XXXI). The theme of *The Brook Kerith*, like that of its forerunner, *Mike Fletcher*, is accordingly 'the growth, the frustration, and finally the renunciation of desire'.[64]

The differences between the two novels, on the other hand, show that between 1889 and 1916 Moore moved from a melodramatic surface Schopenhauerianism to a calmer, more positive, and more truly Schopenhauerian philosophy of life, or, as Michael Brooks puts it, 'One of the major signs of Moore's growth between the work of the Eighties and *The Brook Kerith* is that in the later novel he seems determined to show that pessimism can be interpreted as a wise and humane attitude toward life'.[65] In other words, the recognition that Christ is made to speak with Schopenhauer, means that Schopenhauer's impact on Moore was deeper, more postive, and more lasting than has been generally realized. The point has been well made by Michael Brooks:

> Schopenhauer provided Moore with a framework capable of balancing the two contradictory sides of his complex temperament: a zestful delight in life and a deeply ingrained pessimism. Only in Schopenhauer did Moore find a framework that provided for both the power of the will and its futility. By providing him with his characteristic theme of desire and renunciation, Schopenhauer affected Moore's work deeply and permanently.[66]

It also means that Moore, with Dujardin, has seen more deeply into *The World as Will and Idea* than many of its other readers, probably because of his own ingrained mysticity.

So far as the timing and extent of Moore's knowledge of Schopenhauer is concerned, the evidence of the novels is surprisingly conclusive: by 1885 (writing of *A Drama in Muslin*) he had heard of Schopenhauer, as we know from his review of *A Rebours* in September 1884; by 1886 (writing of *A Mere Accident*) he had already 'looked into' *The World as Will and Idea*. His actual reading of Schopenhauer, which was basically restricted to the all-important Fourth Book of *The World as Will and Idea* in the Haldane-Kemp translation, is most clearly reflected in the *Confessions of a Young Man* (1888, 1889) and *Mike Fletcher* (1889). The title of this Fourth Book — 'The World as Will' — points straight to the idea which is most basic both to Schopenhauer's philosophy and to its impact on Moore's early novels. The last ostensibly 'Schopenhauerian' work he published was the story 'John Norton' (a re-working of *A Mere Accident*) in *Celibates* (1895). And then twenty years later, when Moore's *Schopenhaueriste* phase or pose was very much a thing of the past, there was *The Brook Kerith*, the work in which the influence of Schopenhauer went deepest. Moore's insistance upon the 'oriental' attitude of his Jesus points straight to *The World as Will and Idea* and means that Schopenhauer had long since passed into his bloodstream, although it will have been some time before he realized this, and after the early 1890s he would have been loath to signal the fact.

Though there was virtually nothing of Schopenhauer in it, *Vain Fortune* (1892), we can now see, was the last of a series of novels featuring intellectually or morally impotent characters who are unable to cope with the 'burden of life'. There is a world of difference between *Vain Fortune* and the novel first published only two years later, *Esther Waters*. Unlike Hubert Price, Esther Waters is a simple, energetic character whose instincts are as fundamentally sound as those of her *Schopenhaueriste* predecessors were unsound, and this novel not only 'recreated the English novel' and 'gave us our liberty',[67] but also introduced into Moore's work a striving for philosophical balance that was to persist right through to *Aphrodite in Aulis*.

While it might have been in line with his particularizing cast of mind for Moore to have written novels based on Schopenhauer's philosophy, it would also have been uncharacteristic of him; in any case, with the exception of *Mike Fletcher*, he did not do so. His interest in ideas, though real enough, was too butterfly-like for that. It was presumably because it remained rather scanty that Moore's reading of Schopenhauer impinged so little on his work. It is basic to *Mike Fletcher*, certainly, albeit to the detriment of that work. Otherwise, even in the case of *Confessions*, it was largely a matter of decoration until the Schopenhauer-inspired syncretism and quietism of *The Brook Kerith*. Essentially Moore's 'Schopenhauer-phase', if that is not too grand a term for it, lasted only from 1885 to 1889, and therefore corresponded with the years in which the newly published translation of *The World as Will and Idea* had its greatest impact. Even with reference to these years, however, one can hardly speak of the Schopenhauerian formulas wrought into the web of Moore's narratives as marks of an influence in the strict sense. Moore was simply not 'influenced' by Schopenhauer in the way in which George Gissing, say, was. The Schopenhauerian formulas and echoes in Moore's novels of the latter half of the 1880s may be variously seen as period features, as shock effects, as talismanic utterances, or as ballast. This is, I think, in line with what we know about Moore, who was a pessimist of sorts but not a tragic pessimist.[68] The condition of Ireland had trained him into an attitude of pessimism as early as 1885 (see his articles in *Figaro* that later became *Parnell and his Island*), and in any case his experiences in Paris will soon have taught the impressionable young writer that pessimism was socially and intellectually *de rigeur*. Moore undoubtedly underwent periods of deep disappointment both as man and as writer; he was much less successful as a lover than he would have dreamed of admitting, and precisely during his *Schopenhaueriste* phase was for some years having to face up to continuing artistic failure; but for all that he never seriously despaired of life or of himself. Unlike others of his generation he was never tempted to commit suicide; nor, despite the fact that the quietism of *The Brook Kerith* ran a good deal deeper than his rather stagey surface Protestantism, did he ever take serious refuge in religion. 'The end of life is life,' he wrote to Dujardin in 1903, 'and the only end of art is to help us to live, and as soon as we put our hopes in another world life becomes ugly and art passes out of existence.' It is the 'Zarathoustran' Moore speaking here, and he was probably never more serious in his life. He was in several ways a failure, and at times must have admitted it to himself; but he was too sane and balanced and egotistical a character to have succombed to real despair, which was not his style. That said, the protective shell of his egotism was thin, his balance precarious. He oscillated between self-satisfaction and self-doubt, was both pugnacious and moodily unsure of himself; his irony is both offensive and defensive.

The fact that his preoccupation with Schopenhauer led to a series of novels which — with the exception of *Confessions* — he felt obliged to disclaim as so many aberrations, suggests not only that he was not at home with what he was pleased to call 'the specious sophistries of German philosophers' (*Mike Fletcher*, 10), but also that the novelist needs to keep his eye firmly on the job in hand; it may well have been his experience with Schopenhauerian ideas that made him, quite rightly, 'apprehensive of metaphysical quicksands and mists' (*Avowals*, Chapter 1). He was also, of course, having the sort of bad spell that comes to virtually all writers, though not all preserve the fruits of it; but then

Moore — this is the extraordinary thing about it — thought, at the time, that he was producing some of his best work, so much so that the Norton/Escott/Fletcher material was spread over three novels and a story (another mistake!).

Although he allowed John Norton's Schopenhauerian pessimism to resurface in 1895, by the time of *Evelyn Innes* (1898) Moore was already paraphrasing *Nietzsche*, and it is Nietzsche who is invoked as a tutelary spirit in the Preface to the 1904 edition of the *Confessions* (despite the fact that the Schopenhauer-inspired passages remain unchanged). The visibly 'Schopenhauerian' works were all allowed to fall into oblivion (*A Mere Accident*, *Spring Days*, *Mike Fletcher*), or were expurgated (*A Drama in Muslin*, *Celibates*, *Confessions*), which confirms the modish and in a sense frivolous nature of Moore's early interest in the German pessimist. Schopenhauer was a 'fad' and a good example of what that meant.

It would be easy to conclude that Moore's attitude towards Schopenhauer shows that there is no place for the serious treatment of ideas in the 'aesthetic novel', and with reference to his Schopenhauerian material the conclusion would probably be justified. But it is also easy to underrate George Moore; it is not simply that he is not an ideas man, although he did write in *Confessions* 'let those who have taken firsts at Oxford devote their intolerable leisure to preparing an edition from which everything resembling an idea shall be excluded' (1904 Edn., 255). He may have written to John Eglinton on 4 April 1927 that 'ideas are worthless, yours, mine and everybody else's. Ideas are pernicious',[69] but he was also fascinated by them, and was probably more serious about them than he liked to admit; when he buffoons, it is because he is ashamed to admit that he is serious. Leaving such general considerations aside, the best description I know of the Moore-like man of the 'eighties' is that given by George Gissing in his novel *The Emancipated* (1890):

> One of the characteristics of our time is that it produces men who are determinists by instinct; who, anything but profound students, or subtle reasoners, catch at the floating phrases of philosophy and recognize them as the index of their being, adopt them henceforth as clarifiers of their vague self-consciousness.

This reads for all the world like a description of the man, who, a year earlier, had claimed his philosophy to be 'that of Schopenhauer'. But here too we must not underrate George Moore, who later quoted himself as saying: 'I believe that Schopenhauer was right . . . for surely the sum of our pain exceeds the sum of our pleasures' (*Memoirs of My Dead Life*, VIII: 'The Lovers of Orelay'). And that he meant, or seemed to mean, for these words raise again the central question in George Moore studies: when is Moore being serious?

Be this as the reader will, the context of Moore's last remark is trivial, but, although his work is not without its moments of breathtaking triviality, we have seen that Moore's Schopenhauerism went far beyond the trivial. There is, I think, nothing more serious in Moore's entire *oeuvre* than the quietism and syncretism of *The Brook Kerith*. And those came from Schopenhauer.

III. George Moore and Nietzsche

The *Confessions of a Young Man* reappeared in 1904 with a new Preface which showed Moore nailing a new flag to his mast:

> My Protestant sympathies go back very far, further back than these Confessions . . .
> I find not only my Protestant sympathies in the 'Confessions', but a proud agnosticism, and an exalted individualism which in certain passages leads the reader to the sundered rocks about the cave of Zarathoustra. My book was written before I heard that splendid name, before Zarathoustra was written; and the doctrine, though hardly formulated, is in the 'Confessions', as Darwin is in Wallace. (xv-xvi)

The Preface is a completely new one; the Preface to the third edition of 1889, in which Moore wrote 'I owe much of my mind to Schopenhauer', is not printed, although the references to Schopenhauer in the text all stand. The new Preface shows that by 1904 Moore's enthusiasm for Schopenhauer, overstated in the 1889 edition, is replaced by a defiant anti-Catholicism in the course of which Nietzsche's Zarathustra is invoked. Although Moore's 'Protestant sympathies' were real enough, they also involved an element of anti-Catholic coat-trailing, while the passages in question, probably those in which Pagan Moore damns pity and praises injustice, amount to a rejection of Protestant morality. The *Confessions*, first published in 1888 (after *Also Sprach Zarathustra*), was written well before Moore could have heard of Nietzsche's work. Moore's spelling — 'Zarathoustra' — suggests that his knowledge of Nietzsche came via France, and may mean that he read *Ainsi parlait Zarathoustra* (tr. Henri Albert) when or shortly after it appeared in 1898. That this was probably the case is confirmed by the fact that in summer 1902 John Quinn saw a copy of the French translation of *Zarathustra* on Moore's library table. In a letter to W.B. Yeats dated 27 Sept. 1902 Quinn wrote:

> I mailed to you a week ago my copy of Nietzsche's *Thus Spake Zarathustra* . . . Another reason for my sending it was that I saw a copy of it in the French edition on Moore's library table when I called at his house . . . before I went down to Galway. *If* he is writing a novel on the subject, he may be reading *Zarathustra* with the plan of the novel in his mind.[70]

Quinn's supposition was mistaken. The French spelling recurs in a letter to John Eglinton dated 20 June 1929, where Moore wrote: 'Nietzsche took the name of Zoroaster and improved it very much; Zarathoustra is certainly better'.[71]

The *Confessions of a Young Man* has been called an attempt to introduce 'diabolism' to the English mind, 'diabolism' being both a Victorianism for what Moore called the 'proud agnosticism' of his work, and a word with positively Nietzschean connotations: Bernard Shaw recognized Nietzsche as a fellow-'Diabolonian'. It is therefore likely that John Eglinton's maiden aunt was not alone in regarding George Moore as 'a child of Hell'. Now whatever about his maiden aunt, John Eglinton himself reportedly said that Moore 'caught a good deal' from Nietzsche, while Hone, for his part, quotes Moore's allusion to 'Zarathoustra' in the 1904 Preface, and comments:

> The reference to Nietzsche is interesting, because Moore, as John Eglinton recalls for me, caught a good deal from the German . . . philosopher of whom he had heard much earlier from Dujardin. I myself remember his admiration for his friend, Daniel Halévy's *Vie de Nietzsche*; it was in this way that biography should be written, he said.[72]

Eglinton and Hone were both interested in Nietzsche, so that their evidence is particularly valuable. John Eglinton devoted a chapter of his *Anglo-Irish Essays* of 1917 to 'A Way of Understanding Nietzsche'; while approving of Nietzsche's moral relativism, he criticized the superman-idea as 'a little crazy'. Joseph Hone, biographer of Moore and Yeats, also took an interest in Nietzsche; in addition to translating Halévy's *Vie de Nietzsche* (1909: *The Life of Friedrich Nietzsche*, 1911), he also published an article on 'Nietzsche and Culture' in the *Contemporary Review* in 1914.

Apart from his biographer, Moore had many friends and acquaintances with a keen interest in Nietzsche, including Edouard Dujardin, Daniel Halévy, Téodor de Wyzewa, W.B. Yeats, Arthur Symons, John Eglinton, and Havelock Ellis. More especially, he knew Wyzewa at the time (1891) when he - Wyzewa - was writing the first important article on Nietzsche in French; he was in touch with Havelock Ellis in 1896 and knew *The Savoy*, in which Ellis's historic articles on 'Friedrich Nietzsche' appeared; and he was 're-introduced' to W.B. Yeats in 1902 by John Quinn, who was just then recommending Yeats to read Nietzsche, which Arthur Symons was also doing. Moore could not have failed to hear about Nietzsche, even if he had wanted to.

In all likelihood he had his interest in Nietzsche kindled in Paris, and more particularly in the Rue de la Tour des Dames. It was there that Edouard Dujardin shared with Téodor de Wyzewa a flat at which Moore often stayed on his visits to Paris, while Daniel Halévy lived a few doors away. Moore corresponded with Dujardin (editor of *La Revue Wagnérienne* and *La Revue Indépendante*, and of the newspapers *Fin de Siècle* and *Jean qui Rit*) from November 1886. Dujardin was a man of many passionate enthusiasms; his enthusiasm for Schopenhauer, Wagner and Nietzsche dates from this time, for he was one of the earliest of the French Nietzscheans. Moore himself refers to his friend's enthusiasm for Nietzsche in the early/mid-1890s when he writes in *Conversations in*

Ebury Street (1924, rev. edn. 1930, 179): 'It will never be clear to me whether it was Kant or Nietzsche or Palestinian folk-lore that interrupted the successful administration of *Fin de Siècle*'. In *Hail and Farewell* he refers to Dujardin's habit of invoking Schopenhauer and Nietzsche in the context of discussions about Wagner. Moore therefore may very well have heard about Nietzsche from Dujardin in 1886–87, while he was working on the *Confessions of a Young Man*, which was serialized in the *Revue Indépendante* in 1888.

It was in 1887 that Moore got to know Téodor de Wyzewa, who reviewed *A Mere Accident* in the *Revue Indépendante*. In 1891 Wyzewa published in *La Revue Politique et Littéraire* the article 'Frédéric Nietsche [sic], le dernier métaphysicien' to which I have already referred; this is the article that was to turn John Davidson into a Nietzscheite more or less overnight. While there is no evidence that he did so, Moore probably knew the article, which, coming on top of Dujardin's enthusiasm, may well have prompted him to take an interest in Nietzsche.[73] He certainly took considerable interest in the intellectual life of Paris, and from the early 1890s onwards (as opposed to the mid-1890s onwards in England) Nietzsche's philosophy was discussed in most of the important reviews there. 1891 was also the year in which Moore's friend Arthur Symons visited Germany and made notes in which he referred to 'philosophers from Kant to Nietzsche', and it was the year in which Symons' essay on Odilon Redon appeared in the *Revue Indépendante*. One of the most interesting aspects of Moore's interest first in Schopenhauer and then in Nietzsche is the way in which it involves his closest acquaintances both in Paris and in London. Arthur Symons, whom Moore met in Paris in 1890, also moved in both spheres; he was in Paris on and off from 1889 to 1898 and published in the *Mercure de France*, the periodical which sponsored the first French translation of Nietzsche's works. No doubt Moore's literary Wagnerism was indebted to Arthur Symons as well as to Dujardin.

By 1896 Moore must have found Nietzsche featuring in his literary discussions with Arthur Symons, Havelock Ellis and W.B. Yeats; Edward Martyn, the model for 'John Norton', may also have taken part. Moore was very much involved in early British Nietzscheanism, the most important landmark of which was Havelock Ellis's series of articles ('Friedrich Nietzsche') in *The Savoy* of April, July and August 1896. Now from winter 1893 to 1901 Havelock Ellis lived as a sub-tenant of Arthur Symons in Symons' flat in Fountain Court. George Moore lived nearby at 8 King's Bench Walk. W.B. Yeats lived at Fountain Court (in one of Ellis's rooms) in winter 1895/96; he was still there in January 1896, but left by April, which is when his 'Rosa Alchemica' and the first part of Ellis's Nietzsche-essay appeared in *The Savoy*; in *Vale* Moore refers to

Arthur Symons showing him this number of *The Savoy*. Yeats was therefore living in Havelock Ellis's rooms while Ellis was writing his Nietzsche-essay. Although Yeats's own enthusiasm for Nietzsche only dates from 1902, he must have heard a good deal about Nietzsche from Havelock Ellis in winter 1895/6, as must Arthur Symons and George Moore, both of whom will already have known about Nietzsche from their French connections. Moore and Symons were boon companions at this time. Symons was editor of *The Savoy*, the July 1896 number of which included not only the second part of Havelock Ellis's essay, but also a contribution by George Moore. As a contributor to *The Saturday Review* Arthur Symons will also have read Bernard Shaw's review ('Nietzsche in English') there on 11 April 1896. The first English translations of Nietzsche's works, which appeared in April 1896, inevitably created a stir since they began to make accessible a writer of whom much had been heard on the intellectual grapevine. When Moore, Yeats, Symons and Martyn visited Inishmore together in August 1896 Nietzsche was very much in the air. The first echo of Nietzsche in Moore's work comes in *Evelyn Innes* (1898).

After recalling Moore's admiration of Halévy's Nietzsche-biography, Hone continues:

> Two of the most successful of his paraphrases resulted from this acquaintance, the one at the close of 'Resurgam' (*Memoirs of My Dead Life*) from Nietzsche's poem of the Eternal Return, the other in *Evelyn Innes*, where Ulick Dean bids farewell to the opera singer (the symbol of the two ships which have crossed paths), from Nietzsche's page on 'Stellar Friendship'.[74]

Presumably 'this acquaintance' refers to Moore's acquaintance with Daniel Halévy, whose Nietzsche-biography, *Vie de Nietzsche* (1909 :*The Life of Friedrich Nietzsche*, tr. J.M. Hone, 1911) Moore much admired. Moore does indeed paraphrase a passage from Nietzsche's *The Joyful Wisdom* in *Evelyn Innes*. The English translation of this work did not appear until 1910, and even the French translation (*Le Gai Savoir*, tr. H. Albert) only appeared in 1901, as part of the complete edition of Nietzsche's work begun by the Mercure de France in 1898. It is therefore most likely that Moore first heard of Nietzsche's passage on 'Stellar Friendship' from Daniel Halévy on one of his visits to Paris. Halévy started working on Nietzsche in 1892, and in his *Vie de Nietzsche* he was to quote the passage in question. He probably told Moore about the passage and gave him a French translation of it. Otherwise, Moore could have heard of the passage from Dujardin. Nietzsche's passage summarizes his relationship with Wagner, and it was Wagner who loomed so large both in Dujardin's interests and in *Evelyn Innes*.

If there is some doubt about the source of Moore's knowledge, there is no doubt at all that Ulick Dean's farewell letter echoes Nietzsche. In view of its importance, it must be quoted at length:

> Alas, from our first meeting, and before it, we were aware of the fate which has overtaken us. . . . We are ships, and the destiny of ships is the ocean, the ocean draws us both: we have rested as long as may be, we have delayed our departure, but the tide has lifted us from our moorings. With an agonized heart I watched the sails of your ship go up, and now I see that mine, too, are going aloft, lifted by invisible hands. I look back upon the bright days and quiet nights we have rested in this tranquil harbour. Like ships that have rested a while in a casual harbour, blown hither by storms, we part, drawn apart by the eternal magnetism of the sea . . . In the depths of our consciousness . . . there lies a certain sense that our ways are different ways, and that we must fare forth alone, whither we know not, over the ocean's rim; and in this sense of destiny we must find comfort . . . Ours is the same adventure, though a different breeze fills the sails, though the prows are set to a different horizon . . . But, Evelyn, my heart is aching so . . . the wide ocean which lies outside the harbour is so lonely . . . 'May we not meet again?' my heart cries from time to time; 'may not some propitious storm blow us to the same anchorage again, into the same port?' Ah, the suns and the seas we shall have sailed through would render us unrecognisable, we should not know each other. Last night I wandered by the quays, and, watching the constellations, I asked if we were divided for ever, if, when the earth has become part and parcel of the stars, our love will not re-appear in some starry affinity, in some stellar friendship. (*Evelyn Innes*, 1898, 415f.)

This is a paraphrase of a memorable passage from *The Joyful Wisdom*:

> *Stellar Friendship.* — We were friends, and have become strangers to each other. . . . We are two ships, each of which has its goal and its course; we may . . . cross one another in our paths, and celebrate a feast together as we did before, — and then the gallant ships lay quietly in one harbour and in one sunshine, so that it might have been thought they were already at their goal, and that they had one goal. But then the almighty strength of our tasks forced us apart once more into different seas and into different zones, and perhaps we shall never see one another again, — or perhaps we may see one another, but not know one another again; the different seas and suns have altered us! That we had to become strangers to one another is the law to which we are subject: just by that shall we become more sacred to one another! . . . There is probably some immense, invisible curve and stellar orbit in which our courses and goals, so widely different, may be comprehended as small stages of the way, — let us raise ourselves to this thought! . . . And so we will believe in our stellar friendship. (Section 279).

Even Evelyn's reflections on Ulick Dean's letter derive from Nietzsche:

> The symbol of the ships seemed . . . to express the union and the division and the destiny that had overtaken them . . . in her vision ships hailed each other as they crossed in mid-ocean. Ships drew together as they entered a harbour. Ships separated as they fared forth, their prows set towards different horizons (*Evelyn Innes*, 1898, 416).

The facts of this 'borrowing' speak for themselves. Moore has simply taken Nietzsche's passage and reproduced it bit by bit, expanding and orchestrating it as he does so. The final phrase in Ulick Dean's letter — 'stellar friendship' — points directly to his unacknowledged source. No doubt Moore was attracted to Nietzsche's passage by the fact that it embodies an elaborate version of a metaphor which he had himself used back in 1889 ('I could not bear the thought that you might pass from me. A ship sails away, growing indistinct, and then disappears in the shadows': *Mike Fletcher*, 32). Images of departures for sea voyages are often evoked by Moore when he is moved by the breaking up of human relationships. Although he has improved upon Nietzsche's passage and turned it into the most memorable thing in his own novel, it could be argued that he has not sufficiently improved upon his model to justify borrowing it in this way. The fact that Nietzsche's work was unknown in England at the time may have had something to do with it.

Now Moore again refers to this passage and again uses Nietzsche's metaphor in some revealing lines in *Salve*, where he writes about Father Tom Finlay's *New Ireland Review*, to which he contributed in 1902:

> We shall not meet again, and if we do, of what use? We are like ships; all and sundry have destinies and destinations. There is very little Nietzsche in me, but this much of him I remember, that we must pursue our courses valiantly, come what may. Father Tom and I had lain side by side in harbour for a while, but the magnetism of the ocean drew me, and I continued to write, feeling all the while that my stories were drawing me away from Catholic Ireland. (*Salve*, 1912, 164)

Since he uses it again in this way, Moore must have been pleased with his Nietzschean borrowing in *Evelyn Innes*. In this passage from *Salve* he provides the reference to Nietzsche that had been lacking in the novel, thus proving that the two ships metaphor there does in fact derive from Nietzsche. The self-dramatization in *Salve* is typical of Moore, as it is of Nietzsche, whose work Moore claimed to have largely forgotten by 1912.

This autobiographical passage is one of only two passages in which Moore writes of his own attitude to Nietzsche, and is revealing in that he here casts himself in the role of Nietzsche to Father Tom's Wagner, whereas in *Evelyn Innes* he was using the metaphor from the point of view of his Wagnerian heroine; in view of his affinities with Nietzsche, Moore's self-identification with the German philosopher is not inappropriate. The other passage in question is the 1904 Preface to *Confessions*. The two passages appear to contradict one another, but this is only ostensibly the case, for after denying in *Salve* that there was much Nietzsche in him, he not only borrows a metaphor from the German writer, but repeats that the ideal of full, untrammelled personal development is a conviction that he shares with Nietzsche. This is, moreover, a theme to which Moore continually returned (cf. *The Lake*, *The Untilled Field* and *Reminiscences of the Impressionist Painters*). The expression of that ideal often culminates in images of departure, of ships sailing away, with the coast of the mother-country receding in the distance (The Lake, 'The Wild Goose', 'So on he fares', etc.), because for Moore the ideas of self-development and of exile are closely connected. The Nietzschean image of the two ships leaving harbour for different destinations would thus appeal to him in a very personal way, even without the verbal connexion between 'Stellar Friendship' and 'Stella'.

In 1902 Nietzsche's lines on 'Stellar Friendship' were clearly in Moore's mind, for in an unpublished letter to Mrs Crawford dated 11 Dec. 1902 he asked her for a copy of 'the ten lines that Nietzsche wrote about himself and Wagner in La Gaie Science, "Stellar Friendship". I want the German text.'[75] The way in which Moore puts his request suggests that his knowledge of Nietzsche's lines had been acquired through a French intermediary, possibly Halévy. The French translation of *The Joyful Wisdom* came out in 1901 and was entitled *Le Gai Savoir*. When he quoted 'L'Amitié stellaire' in his *La vie de Frédéric Nietzsche*, Halévy called Nietzsche's book by its 'Italian' subtitle, *La Gaya Scienza*. The title Moore uses is an obvious Frenchification of that, which tends to confirm that Halévy was his source. As to why Moore, in 1902, wanted the German text of the lines he had already paraphrased from the French, the reason is no doubt that his German translator, Max Meyerfeld, wished to base his translation of Moore's paraphrase of Nietzsche as closely as possible on Nietzsche's own words. Meyerfeld was at this time preparing his translation of the revised third edition of *Evelyn Innes* and the revised Tauchnitz edition of *Sister Teresa*, which appeared in 1905 under the title *Irdische und Himmlische Liebe* (2 Vols).

The passage on 'stellar friendship' is the only actual borrowing from Nietzsche in *Evelyn Innes*, but there are a number of minor echoes, some of them very close, most of which are not surprisingly concerned with morality and the relativity of moral values. That typical diabolonian, Sir Owen Asher, makes a distinction between 'conventional' and 'real' morality (68) which is as Nietzschean as the relativism that leads him to the view that 'right and wrong' is 'a question of time and place' (91). Likewise, when Evelyn Innes concludes that 'It is true that man is a moral animal, but it is not true that there is but one morality; there are a thousand' (326), she is making a point which Nietzsche made repeatedly, notably in *Human, All-Too-Human* and *The Joyful Wisdom*. Havelock Ellis summarized Nietzsche's mockery of what Moore calls 'conventional' morality, when he wrote: 'The sphere of the moral is the sphere of tradition . . . To be customary is to be moral, to be individual is to be wicked',[76] and he went on to make Moore's other point: 'Every man must be his own moralist'.[77] Moore knew this passage, which appeared in the July 1896 number of *The Savoy*, which also carried a contribution by himself. No less close to *Human, All-Too-Human* are Evelyn's thoughts on the subject of moral choice:

> Our actions obey an unknown law, implicit in ourselves, but which does not conform

> to our logic. So we very often succeed in proving to ourselves that a certain course is the proper one for us to follow, in preference to another course, but, when it comes for us to act, we do not act as we intended, and we ascribe the discrepancy between what we think and what we do to a deficiency of will power. Man dares not admit that he acts according to his instincts, that his instincts are his destiny. (94)

Evelyn's thoughts touch Nietzsche's at several points, but the main point again concerns *Human, All-Too-Human* (I, i, sect. 57), where Nietzsche argues that moral choice involves the sacrifice of one desire for the sake of gratifying another. A virtual paraphrase of Nietzsche appears in Chapter 9 of Aldous Huxley's *After Many A Summer* (1939), where Mr. Propter says: 'What is commonly called self-sacrifice is the sacrifice of one part of the ego to another part, one set of personal feelings and passions for another set.' Moore's wording does not echo Nietzsche's, but his thought does.

Evelyn's reflections about 'the law which we feel to be right when we look into the very recesses of our soul', of which she thinks 'that these laws seem foolish and illogical when criticized by the light of reason does not prove their untruth' (269), sound very much like Nietzsche's point in *Human, All-Too-Human* (I, i, sect. 31) about the illogical being necessary for man. But even if there is a faint echo of Nietzsche here, her real point, which has to do with religious faith, is quite different from Nietzsche's. *Wholly* in accordance with *Human, All-Too-Human*, however, is Owen Asher's argument that 'when you went to the root of things, no one ever acted except from a selfish motive' (278). The struggle between Owen Asher and Evelyn Innes amounts to that between 'master morality' and 'slave morality', although it must be emphasized that it is not presented as such. Our conclusion must be similar: that the Nietzschean echoes in *Evelyn Innes*, though surely present, are incidental. This is confirmed by the fact that it is Huxley, Darwin and Spencer who surround the negative pole of Evelyn's existence. The source of the echoes of *Human, All-Too-Human* will have been Moore's Nietzschean friends in Paris. Confirmation of the fact that Nietzsche is at times in Owen Asher's mind is found in the continuation of the novel, *Sister Teresa* (1901), in Chapter VI of which Moore makes Owen Asher apostrophize a hawk as 'Verily a thing beyond good and evil, a Nietzschean bird.'

Now let us turn to the *Confessions of a Young Man* in order to see whether the new edition of 1904 does contain 'an exalted individualism which in certain passages leads the reader to the sundered rocks about the cave of Zarathoustra.'

A brief answer would be that it does not. Moore's 'proud agnosticism', it could be argued, clearly derives from Shelley, his 'exalted individualism' from Gautier, and his love of the 'pagan world' from Gautier and Pater.

Thus his words 'I cried "ave" to it all: [the] lust, cruelty [and] slavery [of the pagan world]' (70) sound like Zarathustra's 'pagan' yea-saying to life, but in fact simply show Moore agreeing with Gautier. The new edition of *Confessions* does, however, contain at least two extended passages (131–134, 154–158) which Moore could have had in mind, although it must be said straightaway that most of the possible echoes of Nietzsche there are very indistinct and do not point to *Zarathustra*. It is necessary, then, to treat Moore's claim with caution.

The first passage includes remarks on art and education which are paralleled in Nietzsche's work. Thus 'art is individuality' (131) has many parallels in *The Birth of Tragedy*, and when Moore goes on 'art is the direct antithesis to democracy' (132), this too sounds Nietzschean enough; but in fact it is probably simply a dialectic response to and denial of William Morris's view of art. Moore may or may not have had Nietzsche's view of art in mind at the time; if he did, there is certainly no way of proving it. His emphasis on individuality in art, which certainly parallels Nietzsche's view, is combined with something rather like the transvaluation of values: the artist, Moore says, 'must discover new formulas, new moulds, all the old values must be swept aside, and he must arrive at a new estimate.' These words are taken from Moore's *Reminiscences of the Impressionist Painters* (1906); that they represent his permanent view of art is shown by the fact that they reappear in *Vale*, *Avowals* and *Conversations*. This is very close to what Nietzsche writes in *Zarathustra* about the 'devisers of new values', and yet there is nothing specifically Nietzschean about Moore's words. Nietzsche certainly shared Moore's belief that 'education destroys individuality' (131), but there is no reason to suppose that these words owe anything to Nietzsche either. Both writers, it seems to me, simply shared a horror of what Moore calls 'that menacing figure, Universal Education' (188), which Nietzsche, for his part, regarded as the thin end of the wedge of Communism. Nietzsche was just as convinced as Moore that 'the mass can only appreciate ... conventionalities' (132), but these words of Moore's do not sound as though they reflect a reading of Nietzsche. After all, two writers who are near-contemporaries and are united in their opposition to what they see as the materialism, democratization and vulgarization of life, are likely to have similar views on many subjects. It remains theoretically possible, of course, that all Moore's remarks quoted in this paragraph are connected with Nietzsche in his own mind; the likelihood or otherwise of this being the case can be better judged when we have examined the other extended passage.

Moore goes on, in linked passages which may well owe something to Nietzsche, to bemoan the destruction of 'the great pagan world of marble and pomp and lust and cruelty, that my soul goes out to and hails as the grandest' (155) by the proto-socialist world of Christianity. It is not that his adulation of the 'antique world' is particularly Nietzschean in itself, for his views appear to derive from Pater and Gautier: 'I too am of their [Pater's and Gautier's] company — in this at least [that] I too love the great pagan world, its bloodshed, its slaves, its loathing of all that is feeble' (239). Writers at any given time tend to take similar views of things; and I have already drawn attention to parallels between Pater and Nietzsche on this score.[78] It is, rather, when Moore develops his views on the antique world's 'loathing of all that is feeble' and proceeds to contrast the moralities of the ancient and modern worlds, that his analysis becomes strongly reminiscent of Nietzsche:

> Pity, that most vile of all vile virtues, has never been known to me. The great pagan world I love knew it not. Now the world proposes to interrupt the terrible austere laws of nature which ordain that the weak shall be trampled upon, shall be ground into death and dust, that the strong shall be really strong, — that the strong shall be glorious, sublime . . . Hither the world has been drifting since the coming of the pale socialist of Galilee . . . Come to me, ye who are weak. The Word went forth, the terrible disastrous Word, and before it fell the ancient gods, and the vices they represent, and which I revere, are outcast now in the world of men . . . Thy light, which I, a pagan, standing on the last verge of the old world, declare to be darkness, the coming night of pity and justice which is imminent, which is the twentieth century . . . Injustice we worship; all that lifts us out of the miseries of life is the sublime fruit of injustice . . . Man would not be man but for injustice . . . if mankind does not relinquish . . . its vain, mad and fatal dream of justice, the world will lapse into barbarism . . . Oh, for the antique world, its plain passion . . . the bare, barbarous soul of beauty and of might! (154–159).

Moore wrote, in the same passage, 'What care I that the virtue of some sixteen-year-old maiden was the price paid for Ingres' *La Source*?' This parallels Nietzsche's statement that 'only as artistic material has human life any significance',[79] although the wording is uniquely and shockingly Moore's own. The same applies to Moore's condemnation of pity and praise of injustice, for however close the parallel with Nietzsche — and in this case it is very close — the passages in question are the work of Pagan Moore, for they appeared already in the first (1888) edition of *Confessions*. When they were first expressed in 1888, Moore's pronoucements on the subject of pity and injustice could not possibly have been directly indebted to Nietzsche, although they could conceivably reflect early conversations with Dujardin, and to that extent could be indirectly indebted to *Thus Spake Zarathustra* and *Human, All-Too-Human* respectively. And of course by then Moore could also have heard of what Schopenhauer wrote (in the Fourth Book of *The World as Will and Idea*) of Protestant morality: 'The prevalent and peculiarly Protestant view that the end of life lies solely and immediately in the moral virtues, thus in the practice of justice and benevolence, betrays its insufficiency even in the fact that so miserably little real and pure morality is found among men.' However, I do not think that Moore is echoing Schopenhauer here, for both his context and his tone are very different. On the contrary, the passages seem to me to bear out the truth of Moore's claim in the Preface to the 1904 edition of the *Confessions*, in other words, to confirm that some aspects of Pagan Moore's thought coincided with Nietzsche's, so that there was something of Nietzsche in him long before he had ever heard of Nietzsche. Once he has heard of Nietzsche, he quite naturally draws attention to this fact. For him it was necessary to be *à la mode*; it is because the intellectual public has changed its allegiance that Moore appears to follow suit, although he is hardly doing so. His preference for the 'strong' parallels Nietzsche's views as expressed, particularly, in works from *Human, All-Too-Human* onwards, and is also an expression of the vitalism that is part and parcel of *fin-de-siècle* aestheticism. There is a clear parallel with Yeats's Nietzsche-inspired aristocratic ethic here, and one feels that in Moore's case, as in Yeats's, the appeal of strength is primarily aesthetic. Yeats was interested in Nietzsche partly as a counteractive to the spread of democratic vulgarity. No doubt Moore was too. Instinctively Yeats's sympathies were with the 'strong' rather than the 'weak', with the 'noble' rather than the 'ignoble'; confirmation of this is found in the fact that in Thomas Common's anthology, *Nietzsche as Critic, Philosopher, Poet and Prophet*, which he read with much enthusiasm in 1902, he marked the passage 'The noble man regards *himself* as the determiner of worth.' Further notes in the same volume show that he had no hesitation in accepting Nietzsche's 'Natural System of Ranks and Castes', and that — like Nietzsche himself — he was overridingly concerned with *quality* of life, with perfection in the art of living, with life as an aesthetic phenomenon; but — unlike George Moore — he also had an innate moral conservatism that prevented his aesthetic explorations from going too far.

It is when his glorification of strength is allied to disdain for 'weak' virtues such as pity, that Moore comes closest to Nietzsche, who said that only 'decadent' civilizations regard pity as a virtue, and who wrote in *Thus Spake Zarathustra* (XLIX, LIII): 'So much justice and pity [do I see], so much weakness . . . Pity maketh stifling air for all free souls'. In this case the parallel is so close that Moore may well be echoing Nietzsche, the more so since he goes on 'Man would not be man but for injustice', which accords with the statement in *Human, All-Too-Human* (I, sect. 32) that 'We are from the beginning illogical, and therefore unjust beings'. Moore could have got this particular point from a conversation with Téodor de Wyzewa, who considered *Human, All-Too-Human* to be Nietzsche's most typical work, or he could have read the French translation (*Humain, trop humain*, tr. A.-M. Desrousseaux) which appeared in 1899. The reference to the 'pale socialist of Galilee' comes not from Nietzsche, nor from Heine, but from Swinburne's 'Hymn to Proserpine'. Moore has added the word 'socialist' to Swinburne's 'pale Galilean'. The idea for this addition probably came from a conversation about Nietzsche.

We have seen that *Confessions* does contain passages which parallel Nietzsche, and that one or two of the parallels are close; but there is no *evidence* that any of Moore's pronouncements actually derive from Nietzsche. It is most unlikely that he read much Nietzsche, although he may have taken in a little of his philosophy in a less painful way. Unlike Moore's earlier Schopenhauer paraphrases, the passages in question in *Confessions* are not quotations or near-quotations; far from echoing Nietzsche's wording, Moore's formulations are pallid and abstract by comparison; and in any case the parallel passages are so scattered throughout Nietzsche's work that Moore would have had to read most of it for there to be any question of detailed, first-hand indebtedness. That he did not do so, is quite certain.

Some of his passages probably derive from Nietzsche in a vaguer and more roundabout way, via conversations with Dujardin, Wyzewa, Halévy, Yeats, Symons, Ellis and others. The most Nietzschean of the passages in question, that devoted to the strong and the weak and their respective moralities, almost certainly goes back to Nietzsche in this sort of way. The general impression is that the ideas which Moore liked to see as leading back to 'Zarathoustra' are the fruits of café-society rather than of the study. He will have heard a few heady and attractive ideas attributed to Nietzsche which corresponded with his own ideas; or it may have suited his book to identify them with his own ideas. Given that the ideas in question were almost certainly expressed in French, over a bottle of wine, it is hardly surprising that the echo is indistinct.

The new Preface fully confirms that for Moore truth was a matter of what sounds 'right'. His Prefaces of 1889 and 1904 reflect the cults of Schopenhauer and Nietzsche respectively. In 1904, even more than in 1889, he is attaching the name of his latest fad as a kind of talisman to ideas which are basically unchanged and have little to do with that fad. He is as chameleon-like as ever. But if in 1889 he was merely exaggerating an allegiance to Schopenhauer which did at least exist in his own mind, in 1904 he is inventing an allegiance which never really existed as such, although an affinity did exist. Moore knew something of Nietzsche, had a little in common with him, and chose to paraphrase from his work on occasion; but there is nothing in the 1904 edition of *Confessions* to make one doubt the truth of what he wrote in *Salve*: 'There is very little of Nietzsche in me, but this much of him I remember, that we must pursue our courses valiantly, come what may.' This is the only other passage in his work in which Moore links Nietzsche with himself.

Let us remember, however, that while there was something of Schopenhauer in Moore, there was also an affirmation of life that might not unreasonably be labelled 'Nietzschean', provided the term is understood as meaning parallel to Nietzsche rather than Nietzsche-inspired. This in turn means that there is more truth in Moore's remark about 'Zarathoustra' than there might seem to be. The point has been well made by Jean Noël:

> Il y a en lui une affirmation du vouloir vivre, une volonté de s'imposer qui l'éloignent de Schopenhauer. Ces éléments positifs, joints à un antichristianisme virulent, à un mépris violemment affiché de la pitié, vertu trop chrétienne, à une exaltation du paganisme méditerranéan, de ses cruautés, de ses beautés aussi, font de lui un de ces hommes en qui s'affirme la mentalité "nietzschéenne". Moore ne se trompera pas lorsqu'il écrira en 1904 qu'il y a dans les *Confessions* "un orgueilleux agnosticisme et un individualisme exalté propres à conduire le lecteur parmi les rochers épars autour de la grotte de Zarathoustra.[80]

It must be added that Moore's wording in the 1904 Preface is misleading in that, wishing to claim the talismanic protection of Nietzsche, he gives the impression of having been inspired by Nietzsche, when in fact he serves other, earlier gods.

The other borrowing from Nietzsche noted by Hone comes in a passage from 'Resurgam' at the end of *Memoirs of My Dead Life* (1906):

> What a ceaseless recurrence of the same things! . . . At the end of . . . some billion years, the ultimate moment towards which everything from the beginning has been moving will be reached; and from that moment the tide will begin to flow out again, the eternal dispersal of things will begin again . . . I believe that billions of years hence . . . I shall be sitting in the same room where I sit now, writing the same lines that I am now writing. (11th Edition, 1928, 269f.)

The idea here, though not the wording, echoes the idea which Nietzsche first formulated in *The Joyful Wisdom* (sect. 341):

> This life, as thou livest it at present, and hast lived it, thou must live once more, and also innumerable times; and there will be nothing new in it, but every pain and every joy and every thought and every sigh, and all the unspeakably small and great [things] in thy life must come to thee again, and all in the same series and sequence — and similarly this spider and this moonlight among the trees, and similarly this moment, and I myself. The eternal sand-glass of existence will ever be turned once more, and thou with it, thou speck of dust!

Nietzsche elaborated this idea of eternal recurrence in a famous passage in *Thus Spake Zarathustra* (sect. LVII):

> Everything departs, everything returns; the wheel of existence rolls eternally. All dies, all revives again, the year of existence runs eternally.
>
> All disintegrates, all is integrated anew, the like house of existence builds itself eternally. All separates, all hails itself again; the ring of existence remains true to itself eternally.

Every moment existence begins; round every 'Here' rolls the sphere 'There'. The middle is everywhere. The path of eternity is crooked. ...

Behold, we know what thou teachest: that all things return eternally and we ourselves with them, and that we have already existed times without number and all things with us.

Thou teachest that there is a great year of Becoming, an immensely great year, which, like a sandglass, must ever turn anew, to run down and run out anew. ...

I come again eternally to this identical life, this self-same life ...

We cannot be sure which of Nietzsche's passages Moore is echoing in 'Resurgam'; indeed, his source may be Daniel Halévy, from whom he had already, in all probability, gleaned the passage on 'Stellar Friendship' from *The Joyful Wisdom*. Halévy's book is very much a biography; of Nietzsche's works it is only *Zarathustra* that is discussed and quoted at length. The emphasis is, however, very much on 'Le Retour éternel'. Although he does not quote the passages from *Zarathustra* which Moore's passage in *Memoirs of My Dead Life* recalls, Halévy does quote the words 'Que tout revienne sans cesse' ('Let everything return ceaselessly'), which might be supposed to have given Moore his 'What a ceaseless recurrence of the same things!' And before quoting these words Halévy gave his own description of 'le retour éternel'

Il la trouve enfin, cette idée dont le pressentiment l'agite avec tant de violence. — Un jour qu'il allait à travers bois de Sils-Maria jusqu'à Silvaplana, il s'assit non loin de Surlée au pied d'un rocher pyramidal; à cette minute et à cette place il conçut le Retour éternel. Il pensa: Le temps, dont la durée est infinie, doit ramener, de période en période, une disposition identique des choses. Cela est nécessaire; donc il est nécessaire que toutes choses reviennent. Dans tel nombre de jours, imprévisibile, immense, mais limité, un homme, en tout semblable à moi, moi-même enfin, assis à l'ombre de ce roc, retrouvera ici-même cette même idée. Et cette même idée sera par cet homme retrouvée non pas seulement une fois mais un nombre de fois infini, car ce mouvement qui ramène les choses est infini. Donc nous devons écarter toute espérance et penser fermement: nul monde céleste ne recevra les hommes, nul avenir meilleur ne les consolera. Nous sommes les ombres d'une nature aveugle et monotone, les prisonniers de chaque instant. Mais prenons garde, cette redoutable idée qui nous interdit l'espérance ennoblit et exalte chaque minute de nos vies: l'instant n'est plus une chose passagère, s'il revient éternellement; le moindre est un monument éternel doué de valeur infinie, et, si le mot divin a quelque sens, divine. *'Que tout revienne sans cesse,' écrit-il, 'c'est l'extrême rapprochement d'un monde du devenir avec un monde de l'être: sommet de la meditation.'*[81]

The passage in *Memoirs of My Dead Life* very likely derives from this or from a conversation with Halévy. By 1906 Moore could also have read *Le Gai Savoir* (1901). Or his inspiration could have come from *Ainsi parlait Zarathoustra* (1898) or *Thus Spake Zarathustra* (1896). Be this as it may, it is arguably not the *Confessions*, but this passage from 'Resurgam', which leads the reader back to the sundered rocks about Zarathustra's cave; indeed, it was most likely the fact that *Thus Spake Zarathustra* was so indeed, it was most likely the fact that *Thus Spake Zarathustra* was so talked-about following the appearance of the first English translation in 1896 that tempted Moore into adopting 'Zarathoustra' as his badge or talisman for the 1904 edition of *Confessions*. We have already seen that John Quinn saw a copy of the French translation of *Zarathustra* (*Ainsi parlait Zarathoustra*, 1898) on Moore's library table in summer 1902. Clearly Moore, like Yeats, was preoccupied with Nietzsche in 1902. If the French spelling 'Zarathoustra' suggests that he may have found the myth of eternal recurrence in Paris, it is also possible that he got it from W.B. Yeats, for in summer 1902, when Moore was re-introduced to him by John Quinn, Yeats was reading Common's anthology, which had an immediate and profound effect on him. Yeats was particularly taken with Nietzsche, 'that strong enchanter', as he called him; more especially he was evidently impressed with the vision of eternal recurrence, which was so close to his own vision of things. What more natural than that he should have told Moore of his discovery, the more so since Joseph Hone, in referring to the passage from 'Resurgam', quotes 'Nietzsche's poem of the Eternal Return' as Moore's source. 'The Eternal Return' is the title which is given to the vision of eternal recurrence in Thomas Common's anthology; in *Thus Spake Zarathustra* it bears the chapter heading 'The Convalescent'. It is therefore not unlikely that Moore owed his discovery of this passage to Yeats. Be that as it may, it was Yeats who made profounder use of the passage.

There is an unpublished letter from Moore to Dujardin dated 13 May 1902 in which Moore writes 'Je vous remercie . . . pour Nietzsche . . . Je lis avec plaisir le petit livre sur Nietzsche. J'espère que je lirais ses oeuvres avec la même avidité. Il trouve sa [sic] premier livre mauvais et il a raison.'[82] This is puzzling in that Dujardin's own letter of 2 May 1902, to which Moore is here replying, says nothing about sending Moore a book on Nietzsche, although Moore's letter leaves no doubt that this was the case. When Moore says 'Je vous remercie . . . pour Nietzsche', he may be referring to one or two items. The 'petit livre sur Nietzsche' is possibly, as Jean Noël has suggested to me, P. Lasserre's *La morale de Nietzsche* (Paris, 1902) or Jules de Gaultier's *De Kant à Nietzsche* (Paris, 2nd edn, 1900), although I find it hard to imagine Moore reading either book. *La morale de Nietzsche* contains little that would have been likely to catch Moore's eye, with the possible exception of the phrase 'L'art est l'épanouissement . . . de la morale des maîtres',[83] which corresponds to Moore's 'art is the direct antithesis of democracy' (*Confessions*, 1904 Edn, p. 32). In agreeing that Nietzsche's first book is weak, Moore implies that he has himself read *L'Origine de la tragédie, ou Hellénisme et pessimisme*. I doubt this was the case, although he could have read the French translation (by J. Marnold & J. Morland), which came out in 1901. When Moore goes on to say 'J'espère que je lirais ses oeuvres avec la même avidité', this makes one wonder whether Dujardin did not send or lend Moore one or more volumes of the French edition of Nietzsche's work, and most likely the copy of *Ainsi parlait Zarathoustra* which John Quinn saw on Moore's table in summer 1902. It is also entirely possible that Moore's reference to Nietzsche's 'premier livre' is a reference to the book that Moore mistakenly believed to be Nietzsche's first book: *Ainsi parlait Zarathoustra*

There is, however, another possibility. If Dujardin did send Moore Jules de Gaultier's *De Kant à Nietzsche*, which is possible since Dujardin knew Gaultier, whom he mentioned in his *Le Monologue Intérieur* (1931), then Moore could have found there an interesting passage on Nietzsche's view of art:

> Between grievous reality and his too keen sensibility he interposes the world of plastic representation and here we have Apollinic art . . . By means of Apollinic art the Greeks . . . could enjoy as a spectacle the beauty of the most terrible things . . . What Dionysiac art adds to Apollinic art is the consciousness in the artist of the identity of the spectacle and the spectator. Thereafter man sees himself as the actual creator of all the suffering in which the universe abounds. It is he who endures it, but it is also he who contemplates it, and that is for him the justification of Life. Initiated into the mystery of his identity with all things, the beauty of the drama of life compensates him henceforth for the suffering he assumes as an actor of the representation.[84]

This passage is suggestive in that it makes one wonder whether the Nietzschean idea of art helping man to transcend pessimism, coming on top of 'Art for Art's Sake' and 'Aestheticism', may not have helped Moore to surmount the pessimism of his time. I do not think it safe to assume that Moore knew this particular passage, but he could have obtained a summary of Nietzsche's view of art — which is what Gaultier gives — from Dujardin himself, or from Halévy, or from *L'Origine de la tragédie* (1901) or Thomas Common's *Nietzsche as Critic, Philosopher, Poet and Prophet* (1901). While Common's book will not have been the one sent to Moore by Dujardin, he almost certainly knew it. If he had the book in his hands, he would have been likely to turn to the section on 'Aesthetics', and there he would at once have found Nietzsche's basic view of art:

> only as an *aesthetic phenomenon* is existence and the world eternally justified . . . Only in so far as the genius, in the act of artistic production, coalesces with the primordial artist of the world does he get a glimpse of the eternal essence of art; for in this state he is in a marvellous manner like the weird picture in the fairy-tale, which can at will turn its eyes and behold itself; he is now simultaneously subject and object, poet, actor, and spectator . . .

Not only is this rather more eye-catching than anything Moore might have found in Gaultier, but it is followed, almost immediately, by Nietzsche's famous passage on 'L'Art pour l'art':

> The hostility to the end in art is always hostility to the *moralising* tendency in art, to its subordination under morality. *L'art pour l'art* means: 'The devil take morality!' — But this hostility itself still betrays the domination of prejudice. When the ends of the ethical preacher and the improver of mankind have been excluded from art, it still does not by any means follow that art generally is without an end, without a goal, without meaning; in short, *l'art pour l'art* — a serpent which bites its own tail. 'No end at all, rather than a moral end!' is what mere passion says. A psychologist, on the other hand, asks: What does art do? Does it not praise? Does it not glorify? Does it not select? Does it not bring into prominence? In all these cases it *strengthens* or *weakens* certain estimates of worth. Is this only a contingent matter? an accident? something with which the instinct of the artist should not be at all concerned? Or rather, is it not the prerequisite which *enables* the artist to do something? Is his fundamental instinct concerned with art, or is it not rather concerned with the significance of art, namely, *life? a desirableness of life?* — Art is the great stimulus to life; how could it be understood as purposeless, as aimless, as *l'art pour l'art*?[85]

In my view Moore is both likelier to have known Common's book than Gaultier's, and would have found this last passage much more stimulating than anything in Gaultier. What Nietzsche does, after all, is first to give a powerful justification of art in terms which would appeal to Moore, and then to give the idea of 'art for art's sake' a highly positive meaning. Had he read them, these two passages must surely have helped Moore to transcend pessimism. Is not the view of art adopted by Moore in his *Reminiscences of the Impressionist Painters* (1906) close to Nietzsche's view? Moore said there that

> without courage there cannot be Art . . . All conventions . . . must be cast into the melting-pot; he who would be an artist must melt down all things; he must discover new formulas, new moulds, all the old values must be swept aside, and he must arrive at a new estimate. The artist should keep himself free from all creed, from all dogma, from all opinion . . . all his feelings and . . . ideas must be his own, for Art is a personal re-thinking of life from end to end, and for this reason the artist is always eccentric. He is almost unaware of your moral codes . . . Art is but praise of life, and it is only through the arts that we can praise life. (In: *Hail and Farewell*, ed. R. Cave, 1976, 650f, 663)

A similar view of art is found in *Avowals* and *Conversations*. While this view is not necessarily indebted to Nietzsche, it is a fact that Moore expresses not only Nietzsche's view of art, but his view of the ideal freethinker — which emphasizes again the affinity between Moore and Nietzsche, both of them *enfants terribles* given to overstatement of sufficient truths.

Compared with Schopenhauer's, Nietzsche's impact on George Moore was minimal. We have seen that John Eglinton's reported statement that Moore 'caught a good deal' from Nietzsche, is not confirmed by an examination of the facts. Eglinton was interested in Nietzsche, and Moore, who put himself out to impress Eglinton, who was very useful to him, may have feigned an exaggerated interest in Nietzsche for the younger writer's benefit. No doubt Moore was interested in Nietzsche in a general way; by the time he met Eglinton in 1898, he had, after all, lived through French Nietzscheism and was experiencing the British variety. Nietzsche was so much in the air that Moore could not have avoided him, even if he had wanted to, which is unlikely, for he delighted in 'naughty' ideas, of which Nietzsche was considered the epitome. It is highly likely, especially in view of the occasional presence there of W.B. Yeats and John Eglinton, that some of the ideas which were thrown about at Moore's Saturday evening at-homes in Dublin in the first decade of the century were Nietzschean ones.[86]

The first book by George Moore that is demonstrably indebted to Nietzsche is *Evelyn Innes* (1898). There and in *Memoirs of My Dead Life* (1906) Moore paraphrases Nietzsche. The main paraphrase is used again in *Salve*. It is a curious fact that Moore used Nietzsche as a kind of emotional crutch when writing about parting and death. *Evelyn Innes* also contains what seem to be a number of minor echoes of *Human, All Too Human*. So far as the 1904 edition of *Confessions* is concerned, Moore's comment that 'certain passages' there 'lead the reader to . . . Zarathoustra' needs to be taken with a pinch of salt; the fact is that there are some passages which could be, but none which need be Nietzschean. The 'Zarathoustran' passages in the book echo the ideas of the late 1880s in general, which tend to sound 'Nietzschean': André Gide found Nietzsche less exciting than he expected because he had already read Oscar Wilde, and Thomas Mann too noted how many of Nietzsche's aphorisms might have been written by Wilde (and vice versa). To speak of any significant indebtedness to Nietzsche on Moore's part would be wrong. Moore borrowed ideas and metaphors wherever he could find them. A few happened to come from Nietzsche.

A young man starting to write novels in the 1870s or early 1880s was pretty well bound to go through a pessimistic phase and could hardly fail to be influenced by the unholy trinity of German pessimism (Schopenhauer, Hartmann, Nietzsche). This was the case with George Moore, as it was with Thomas Hardy and (take away Hartmann) with George Gissing. Moore's remarks in the *Confessions of a Young Man* about the 'odious pessimism' of Flaubert and the 'horrors of pessimism' as such do not alter the facts which the present brief study has revealed. There may have been 'very little Nietzsche' in George Moore, but for a time there was not a little Schopenhauer.

Notes

[1] Quoted from R.-P. Colin, *Schopenhauer en France*, Lyon, 1979, 132.
[2] F. Brunetière published a later article, 'La philosophie de Schopenhauer' (*Revue des deux mondes*, Oct. 1886, 694–706), which Thomas Hardy is said to have read.
[3] Writing under the pseudonym 'Labruyère'.
[4] Jean Lorrain (writing under the pseudonym 'Bruscambille'), 'Les schopenhauerdeurs', *L'Evènement*, 20 Sept. 1888.
[5] Millaud, loc. cit.
[6] Rémy de Gourmont, *Promenades Littéraires*, 4e série, 1920, 71.
[7] Colin, 207.
[8] See Colin, 204.
[9] Reprinted in Maupassant's *Chroniques littéraires et chroniques parisiennes.*
[10] Quoted from Colin, 202.
[11] Schopenhauer, *Pensées, maximes et fragments*, ed. J. Bourdeau, 1880, 38f.
[12] Joseph Hone, *The Life of George Moore*, 1936, 74.
[13] In *Lettres inédites à Emile Zola*, ed. C.A. Burns, Paris, 1958; quoted by Colin, 157.
[14] MS B.N. N.A.F. 10 311; quoted from Colin, 168.
[15] Ibid., 175.
[16] In: J.-K.Huysmans, *Lettres inédites à Emile Zola*, ed. P. Lambert & P. Cogny, Geneva, 1953, 100, note 3.
[17] T.G. West, 'Schopenhauer, Huysmans and French Naturalism', *Journal of European Studies*, Dec. 1971, 317.
[18] Huysmans, *Lettres inédites à Emile Zola*, ed. Lambert & Cogny, 99.
[19] Quoted from Colin, 176.
[20] Quoted from Colin, 184.
[21] R. Kuhn, *The Demon of Noontide: Ennui in Western Literature*, Princeton, 1976, 322–326.
[22] R. Baldick, *The Life of J.-K. Huysmans*, Oxford, 1955, 68f.
[23] Ibid., 354.
[24] Hone, 119.
[25] Quoted from Jean C. Noël, *George Moore. L'homme et l'oeuvre*, Paris, 1966, 143.
[26] M. Steward, 'J.-K. Huysmans and George Moore', *Romanic Review*, XXV, July 1934, 199.
[27] R. Baldick, 88.
[28] R. Baldick, in the Introduction to his translation of *A Rebours: Against Nature*, 1959, 11.
[29] In a letter to his brother Julian; see Hone, 131.
[30] G.A. Cevasco, 'Something Exquisite and Spiritous: J.-K. Huysmans and George Moore', *Research Studies*, XLV, Sept. 1977, 147–159.
[31] Quoted from Colin, 190.
[32] Ibid.
[33] Ibid., 192.
[34] T.G. West, 322.
[35] Ibid., 323.
[36] Schopenhauer, *The World as Will and Idea* tr. Haldane & Kemp, 7th ed, n.d. 349–532.
[37] *WWI*, Vol. III.
[38] *W.B. Yeats and T. Sturge Moore. Their Correspondence 1901–1937, ed. Ursula Bridge, 1953, 117f.*
[39] D. Halèvy, *La vie de Frédéric Nietzsche*, Paris, 1909, 34.
[40] See: M. Brown, *George Moore: A Reconsideration*, Seattle, 1955, 77.
[41] Oscar Wilde, *Letters*, ed. R. Hart-Davis, 1962, 20.
[42] E.g. in *Spring Days*, 1888, 313f.
[43] Jean C. Noël, 127.
[44] Susan Mitchell, *George Moore*, Dublin, 1916, 103.

[45] A few years earlier, in 1882, George Gissing had begun his novel *The Unclassed*, the original title of which was *The Burden of Life*. The novel is based on Schopenhauer; see my *Gissing and Germany*, 1981, 49ff.

[46] Quoted from Hone, 14.

[47] Moore, *Confessions of a Young Man*, ed. Susan Dick, 1972, 250; the Wagner quotation is from Richard Wagner, *Prose Works*, tr. W.A. Ellis, New York, 1966, V, 70.

[48] Hone, 141f.

[49] Page 383.

[50] I gratefully adopt the metaphor which Jean Noël used in a letter to me.

[51] A. Farrow, *George Moore*, 1978, 80.

[52] Ibid., 83.

[53] 'Who was that lad they used to try to make me read at Oxford? Ship— Shop— Schopenhauer. That's the name. A grouch of the most pronounced description.' (P.G. Wodehouse, *Carry on, Jeeves*, Chapter 9).

[54] F. Bowen, *Modern Philosophy from Descartes to Schopenhauer and Hartmann*, 1877, 430. *If* he read the book, Moore would no doubt have been struck by Bowen's statement that 'Alone . . . among all ancient or modern philosophers, he is an avowed, consistent, and thorough-going Pessimist. To him, this is the worst of all possible worlds, tenanted by the worst of all possible beings, mankind' (413); but it is unlikely that he read this rather dry and academic work.

[55] M.W. Brooks, 'George Moore, Schopenhauer, and the Origins of *The Brook Kerith*', *English Literature in Transition*, XII, 1969, 23.

[56] Quoted from Hone, 379.

[57] Quoted from Hone, 161.

[58] See: *Letters of George Moore*, ed. John Eglinton, n.d., 40.

[59] A. Farrow, 86.

[60] On Moore and Wagner, see Wm F. Blissett ('George Moore and Literary Wagnerism', *Comparative Literature*, XIII, 1961, 52–71) and Max Moser (*Richard Wagner in der englischen Literatur des XIX, Jahrhunderts*, Berne, 1938, 89–98). Blissett is as good on Moore's successive discovery first of French literary Wagnerism and then of Wagner and his music, as he is on the 'swirl of Wagnerian situations' in *Evelyn Innes*.

[61] Hone, 142.

[62] M. Brown, 211f.

[63] *Letters of George Moore*, ed. Eglinton, 83.

[64] M.W. Brooks, 24.

[65] Ibid.

[66] Ibid, 21.

[67] Charles Morgan, *Epitaph on George Moore*, 1935, 2.

[68] The rest of this paragraph is much indebted to Jean Noël.

[69] *Letters of George Moore*, ed. John Eglinton, n.d., 71.

[70] For John Quinn's letter to W.B. Yeats of 27 Sept. 1902, see *Letters to W.B. Yeats*, ed. Finneran, Harper & Murphy, I, 1977, 106.

[71] *Letters of George Moore*, ed. Eglinton, 83.

[72] Hone, 257.

[73] By the same token Moore may have known the slightly later article by the principal French translator of Nietzsche's works, Henri Albert: 'Friedrich Nietzsche', *Mercure de France*, VII, 1893, 46–64, 163–173. Presumably this article inspired Havelock Ellis's series of articles in *The Savoy*.

[74] Hone, 257f.

[75] In the National Library of Ireland (MS 2645, Letters of George Moore to Mrs Crawford). I am grateful to Jean Noël for drawing my attention to this letter.

[76] 'Friedrich Nietzsche, II', *The Savoy*, No. 3, July 1896, 77.

[77] Ibid., 79.
[78] In my *Nietzsche in Anglosaxony*, 1972, 21–29.
[79] I quote George Gissing's paraphrase of Nietzsche from *The Unclassed* (1884).
[80] Noël, 159.
[81] Halévy, 233f.
[82] Quoted from a transcription by Jean Noël, to whom I am again indebted.
[83] P. Lasserre, *La morale de Nietzsche*, Paris, 1902, 70.
[84] Jules de Gaultier, *From Kant to Nietzsche*, tr. G.M. Spring, 1961, 234f.
[85] Thomas Common, *Nietzsche as Critic, Philosopher, Poet and Prophet*, 1901, 141f, 145f.
[86] I must add, however, that neither Susan Mitchell (op. cit.) nor John Eglinton ('Recollections of George Moore', in his *Irish Literary Portraits*, 1935) so much as mentions Nietzsche, which is surprising since Hone quoted Eglinton as saying that Moore 'caught a good deal' from Nietzsche.

Bibliography

Note: Unless stated otherwise, English books are published in London, French books in Paris.

Albert, Henri — 'Friedrich Nietzsche', *Mercure de France*, VII, 1893, 46–64, 163–173.

Alexis, Paul — 'L'Amour', *Le Réveil*, 5 August 1883.
Le Besoin d'Amour, 1885.

Baldick, R. — The Life of J.-K. Huysmanns, Oxford, 1955.

Blissett, Wm F. — 'George Moore and Literary Wagnerism', *Comparative Literature*, XIII, 1961, 52–71.

Bowen, Francis — *Modern Philosophy from Descartes to Schopenhauer and Hartmann*, 1877.

Bridge, U. (Ed.) — *W.B. Yeats and T. Sturge Moore. Their Correspondence 1901–1937*, *1953*.

Bridgwater, Patrick — *Nietzsche in Anglosaxony*, Leicester, 1972.
H.G. Wells and Nietzsche, 1980.
Gissing and Germany, 1981.
'English Writers and Nietzsche', in *Nietzsche: Imagery and Thought*, ed. M. Pasley, 1978, 220–258.

Brooks, M.W. — 'George Moore, Schopenhauer, and the Origins of *The Brook Kerith*,' *English Literature in Transition*, XII, 1969, 21–31.

Brown, Malcolm — *George Moore: A Reconsideration*, Seattle, 1955.

Brunetière, F. — (Review of Elme Caro, *Le pessimisme au XIXe siècle*) *Revue des Deux Mondes*, 15 January 1879 (re. 'le Schopenhauerismus').
'La philosophie de Schopenhauer', *Revue des Deux Mondes*, 1 October 1886.

Bruscambille — see Lorrain, J.

Caro, Elme — *Le pessimisme au XIXe siècle*, 1878.

Céard, Henry — 'Arthur Schopenhauer', *L'Express*, 8 August 1881.
'Clowns at philosophes', *Le Siècle*, 19 October 1888.
Lettres inédites à Emile Zola, ed. C.A. Burns, 1958.

Cevasco, G.A. — 'Something Exquisite and Spiritous: J.-K. Huysmans and George Moore', *Research Studies*, XLV, 1977, 147–159.

Colin, René-Pierre — *Schopenhauer en France*, Lyon, 1979.

Eglinton, John — *Anglo-Irish Essays*, 1917.
Irish Literary Portraits, 1935.

Ellis, Havelock — 'Friedrich Nietzsche', *The Savoy*, April/July/August 1896.

Farrow, A. — *George Moore*, 1978.

Finneran, R.J. et al. — *Letters to W.B. Yeats*, I, 1978.

Gaultier, Jules de — *From Kant to Nietzsche*, tr. G.M. Spring, 1961.

Gissing, George — *The Unclassed*, 1884.
The Nether World, 1889.

Gourmont, Rémy de — *Proménades Littéraires*, 4e série, 1920.

Halévy, Daniel — *La vie de Frédéric Nietzsche*, 190 (= *The Life of Friedrich Nietzsche*, tr. J.M. Hone, 1911).

Hartmann, Eduard von — *Philosophie de l'inconscient*, tr. D. Nolen, 1877.
Philosophy of the Unconscious, tr. W.C. Coupland, 3 vols., 1884.
'L'école de Schopenhauer', *Revue philosophique*, August 1883.

Hone, Joseph — 'Nietzsche and Culture', *Contemporary Review*, CVI, 1914, 674–680.
The Life of George Moore, 1936.

Hueffer, Francis — 'Arthur Schopenhauer', *Fortnightly Review*, December 1876, 773–792.
'The Literary Aspects of Schopenhauer's Work', *New Quarterly Magazine*, VIII, 1877, 357–378.

Huysmans, J.-K. — *En Ménage*, 1881.
A Vau l'Eau, 1882.
A Rebours, 1884 (= *Against Nature*, tr. R. Baldick, 1959).
En Route, 1895.
Lettres inédites à Emile Zola, ed. P. Lambert & P. Cogny, Geneva, 1953.

Kuhn, R. — *The Demon of Noontide: Ennui in Western Literature*, Princeton, 1976.

Labruyère — see Millaud, A.

Lasserre, P. — *La morale de Nietzsche*, 1902.

Lichtenberger, H. — *La philosophie de Nietzsche*, 1898.

Lorrain, J. — 'Les schopenhauerdeurs', *L'Evènement*, 20 September 1888.

Maupassant, Guy de — 'La Lysistrata moderne', *Le Gaulois*, 30 December 1880.
'Le Verrou', *Gil Blas*, 25 July 1882.
'Auprès d'un Mort', *Gil Blas*, 30 January 1883.
Bel Ami, 1886.
Sur l'Eau, 1888.
Chroniques littéraires et chroniques parisiennes, n.d.

Millaud, Albert — 'Le Schopenhaueriste', *Le Figaro*, 21 March 1886.

Mitchell, Susan — *George Moore*, Dublin, 1916.

Moore, George — *A Modern Lover*, 1883.
A Mummer's Wife, 1885.
A Drama in Muslin, 1886.
A Mere Accident, 1887.
Spring Days, 1888.
Confessions of a Young Man, 1888 (ed. Susan Dick, 1972).
Mike Fletcher, 1889.
'Some of Balzac's Minor Pieces', *Fortnightly Review*, 1 October 1889.
Celibates, 1895.
Evelyn Innes, 1898.
Sister Teresa, 1901.
Reminiscences of the Impressionist Painters, 1906.
Memoirs of My Dead Life, 1906.
Hail and Farewell, 3 vols., 1911–14 (ed. R. Cave, 1976).
The Brook Kerith, 1916.

Avowals, 1919.
Conversations in Ebury Street, 1924.
Letters of George Moore, ed. John Eglinton, Bournemouth, [1942].

Morgan, C. — *Epitaph on George Moore*, 1935.

Moser, Max — *Richard Wagner in der englischen Literatur des XIX. Jahrhunderts*, Berne, 1938.

Nietzsche, Friedrich — *A travers l'oeuvre de Frédéric Nietzsche*, ed. P. Lauterbach & A. Wagnon, 1893.
Nietzsche as Critic, Philosopher, Poet and Prophet, ed. T. Common, 1901.
Thus Spake Zarathustra, tr. A. Tille, 1896.
Ainsi parlait Zarathoustra, tr. H. Albert, 1898.
Humain, trop humain tr. A.-M. Desrousseaux, 1899.
Human, All-Too-Human, tr. H. Zimmern, 1909.
Le Gai Savoir, tr. H. Albert, 1901.
The Joyful Wisdom, tr. T. Common, 1910.
L'Origine de la tragédie, ou Hellènisme et pessimisme tr. J. Marnold & J. Morland, 1901.
The Birth of Tragedy, or Hellenism and Pessimism, tr. W.A. Haussmann, 1909.

Noël, Jean C. — *George Moore. L'homme et l'oeuvre*, 1966.

Oxenford, John — 'Iconoclasm in German Philosophy', *Westminster Review*, April 1853, 388–407.

Pailleron, Edouard — *Le Monde où l'on s'ennuie*, 1881.

Ribot, Théodule — *La philosophie de Schopenhauer*, 1874.

Schopenhauer, Arthur — 'Metaphysique d'amour', tr. A. Maillard, *Revue Germanique*, 31 January 1861.
Essai sur le libre-arbitre, tr. S. Reinach, 1877.
The Will in Nature, tr. P. Eckler, N.Y., 1877.
Le fondement de la morale, tr. A. Burdeau, 1879.
Pensées, maximes et fragments, tr. J. Bourdeau, 1880.
Aphorismes sur la sagesse dans la vie, tr. J.A. Cantacuzène, 1880.
Select Essays, tr. G. Droppers & C.A.P. Dachsel, Milwaukee, 1881.
The World as Will and Idea, tr. R.B. Haldane & J. Kemp, 3 vols., 1883–86.
Le Monde comme Volonté et comme Représentation, tr. J.A. Cantacuzène, 2 vols., 1886.
Le Monde comme Volonté et comme Représentation, tr. A. Burdeau, 3 vols., 1888–90.
Parerga und Paralipomena, 2 vols., Berlin, 1851.

Shaw, Bernard — 'Nietzsche in English', *The Saturday Review*, 11 April 1896.

Steward, M. — 'J.K. Huysmanns and George Moore', *Romanic Review*, XXV, 1934, 197–206.

Sully, James — *Pessimism*, 1877 (= *Le Pessimisme*, tr. A. Bertrand & P. Gérard, 1882).

West, T.G. — 'Schopenhauer, Huysmanns and French Naturalism', *Journal of European Studies*, 1971, 313–324.

Wilde, Oscar	*Letters*, ed. R. Hart-Davis, 1962.
Wodehouse, P.G.	*Carry on, Jeeves*, 1925.
Wyzewa, Téodor de	'Frédéric Nietsche [sic], le dernier métaphysicien', *La Revue Politique et Littéraire*, XLVIII, 1891, 586–592.
Zimmern, Helen	*Arthur Schopenhauer. His Life and his Philosophy*, 1876.
Zola, Emile	*La Joie de Vivre*, 1884.